D1084567

Essays and Studies 1995

The English Association

The objects of the English Association are to promote the knowledge and appreciation of the English language and its literature, and to foster good practice in its teaching and learning at all levels.

The Association pursues these aims by creating opportunities of co-operation among all those interested in English; by furthering the recognition of English as essential in education; by discussing methods of English teaching; by holding lectures, conferences, and other meetings; by publishing journals, books, and leaflets; and by forming local branches.

Publications

The Year's Work in English Studies. An annual bibliography. Published by Blackwell.

The Year's Work in Critical and Cultural Theory. An annual bibliography. Published by Blackwell.

Essays and Studies. An annual volume of essays by various scholars assembled by the collector covering usually a wide range of subjects and authors from the medieval to the modern. Published by D.S. Brewer.

English. A journal of the Association, *English* is published three times a year by the Association.

The Use of English. A journal of the Association, *The Use of English* is published three times a year by the Association.

Newsletter. A *Newsletter* is published three times a year giving information about forthcoming publications, conferences, and other matters of interest.

Benefits of Membership

Institutional Membership

Full members receive copies of *The Year's Work in English Studies, Essays and Studies,* English (3 issues) and three *Newsletters.*

Ordinary Membership covers *English* (3 issues) and three *Newsletters.*

Schools Membership includes copies of each issue of *English* and *The Use of English,* one copy of *Essays and Studies,* three *Newsletters,* and preferential booking and rates for various conferences held by the Association.

Individual Membership

Individuals take out Basic Membership, which entitles them to buy all regular publications of the English Association at a discounted price, and attend Association gatherings.

For further details write to The Secretary, The English Association, The University of Leicester, University Road, Leicester, LE1 7RH.

Essays and Studies 1995

The Endings of Epochs

Edited by
Laurel Brake

for the English Association

D. S. BREWER

ESSAYS AND STUDIES 1995
IS VOLUME FORTY-EIGHT IN THE NEW SERIES
OF ESSAYS AND STUDIES COLLECTED ON BEHALF OF
THE ENGLISH ASSOCIATION
ISSN 0071–1357

First published 1995
D. S. Brewer, Cambridge

D. S. Brewer is an imprint of Boydell & Brewer Ltd
PO Box 9, Woodbridge, Suffolk IP12 3DF, UK
and of Boydell & Brewer Inc.
PO Box 41026, Rochester, NY 14604–4126, USA

ISBN 0 85991 474 7

British Library Cataloguing-in-Publication Data
Endings of Epochs. – (Essays & Studies
Series, ISSN 0071–1357;Vol.48)
I. Brake, Laurel II. Series
809
ISBN 0–85991–474–7

The Library of Congress has cataloged this serial publication:
Catalog card number 36-8431

This publication is printed on acid-free paper

Printed in Great Britain by
St Edmundsbury Press Ltd, Bury St Edmunds, Suffolk

Contents

Preface

Kinney was the cook. . . . Wherever he went, he carried or found adversity; but with a heart fed on the metaphysics of Horace Greeley, and buoyed up by a few wildly interpreted maxims of Emerson, he had always believed in other men, and their fitness for the terrestrial millennium, which was never more than ten days or ten miles off. (W.D. Howells, A Modern Instance (1882), Signet: New York, 1964, pp. 96–7)

This wry, easy and comedic invocation of 'the terrestrial millennium' is as uncharacteristic of millennial discourses as it is of the determinist novel of which it is a part. But the chiaroscuro of the whole, the co-presence of lurid lights and shadows, does deliver what may be regarded as the characteristic, oxymoronic structure of such discourses, from the 'fortunate fall' onwards: hope constrained by fear.

Nowadays in Britain we talk about 'managing change' and not endings; there is no paradise lost or to come, only the recurrent miracle of birth, the possibilities of love and work, and inevitable death, a trajectory increasingly confined to articulation in terms of the private sphere. Convincing public rhetoric or eschatologies of peaceful transformation or change are rare in British political and intellectual life, displaced by those of individualism and nationalism. While the destruction of the Berlin Wall and the breakdown of the Soviet Union were alleged to prefigure the rebirth of the individual consumer in the paradise of the advanced capitalist state, the carnage in Bosnia and the passivity of the international spectators reveal both the emptiness of that rhetoric taken in isolation, and the power of other competing and apparently ineradicable ideologies. The conundrum of 'Bosnia' re-enforces the terrific fear that still accompanies the millennial structure of apocalyptic change, detached as it now is from the guarantee of Divine Justice in The Last Judgement. The freeing of Nelson Mandela and the achievement of the new South Africa stand out in Britain in the 1990s as rare symbols of large scale and fundamental change, signs of paradise (re)gainable, if not (re)gained. More typical of our national culture is the National Lottery, which functions literally as as agent of apocalyptic and, significantly, material change, and figuratively as the sign of the fate of the subject – winners and bidders – amidst the debris of the welfare state.

Primarily we are left to look to the arts, popular culture, and technology, to the ludic play of postmodern experience – from painting to
video, paperbacks to CDs, the Channel Tunnel to the net – for
paradigms of transformation which gesture towards perfection and to
seek out the muted manifestos of minority groups, such as the greens.
Yet even as we do, the partiality and tentativeness of the invocations
and the plethora of visions attest to the conditions of the post- struc-
turalist world: the end (or weakness) of the grand narratives and of the
unified subject. These are the conditions of mid 1990s culture inscribed
in the writing that follows – diversity of approach within as well as
between pieces, tentativeness, multiple and layered outcomes, and
pleasure in textuality.

The three essays here which address the work of contemporary
authors, by Margaret Beethem, Penny Smith, and Jeremy Green,
discuss grotesqueries of the dance of death in Alasdair Gray's *Lanark*,
Martin Amis's *London Fields*, and Don DeLillo's *Mao II*, as well as
structures of hope in Angela Carter's *Nights at the Circus*, Donna
Haraway's 'A Cyborg Manifesto', bell hooks' *Outlaw Culture*, and
Shena Mackay's *Dunedin*. Gothic, defensive, virulent, and from the
margins as these tend to be, they are innovative and influential con-
testations of trajectories of decline, inscribed in discourses attaching to
the public sphere as well as in literary language and form, and the
individual speaking subject; feminism, gender, ethnicity, popular culture, science fiction and detective fiction figure in this writing as
formations of transformation.

The cluster of essays here referring to the late nineteenth century, by
Joe Bristow, Laurel Brake, and Margaret Beetham, read writing from
the period largely in terms of the problematic of gendered desire, with
Bristow exploring perversity or the oscillation between aesthetic and
erotic topoi in Arthur Symons's poetry of male heterosexuality, Brake
gender dimensions of the *Yellow Book*, a story by Henry James, and the
new journalism, and Beetham apocalypse and utopia in nineteenth-
century feminism, in the press of the period as well as in Sylvia
Townsend Warner's utopian text, *Dreams*.

The Ending of Epochs begins with the seventeenth century, a period
characterised by contesting if interlocking grand narratives and by the
publication of *Paradise Lost*, the assertive inscription in English of a
Protestant reading of the story of the 'first' ending of epochs. Opening
the volume, Helen Wilcox sets Milton's poem in the midst of writing
by Donne, Marvell, Herbert, and An Collins which typically articulates
desire for the Last Judgement, and the Revelation and rebirth which

succeed it, of which it is a necessary precedent. Ending gives way to 'an
"endless" future'.

To map the twin vision of ending and beginning of Paradise Lost,
Wilcox invokes King Lear's 'Is this the promis'd end?/ Or image of that
horror?' (5.3.262–3). Developed and played out in seventeenth-
century drama, the grand narratives are constitutive of the dramatic
representation of an assortment of epochs, situated around Church,
State, monarchs, and men and women. In Gordon McMullan's piece
on Shakespeare and Fletcher's Henry VIII, he also frees the ending of
epochs from its calendar definition and extends it – to both the reading
of 'late,' testamentary work, and the eschatology and historiography of
history, in understanding the play's treatment of 'the end of history' as
the triumph of Protestantism at a moment of contemporary uncertainty
about that claim.

In Beloved, Tony Morrison's contemporary epitaph of the epoch of
slavery in America, the murderous violence of the past is rewritten,
with agency transferred from white male/master to black slave/mother,
and meaning transformed from enslavement to liberation. Asserting
the living memory of slavery in our century, and embedding and
materialising it in history, Morrison invokes the seventeenth-century
construction of the fortunate fall twice over, both in Sethe's murder of
her infant daughter, and in the plot of Beloved's ghostly rebirth,
telescopic life, and assent to death, which frees both her own spirit and
that of Sethe, Paul D and future generations: 'It was not a story to pass
on' (275). The extent to which Morrison's late twentieth-century
secular fable is comedic – ultimately, and just upbeat, is attributable in
no small part to its ideological roots in the politics of black empower-
ment, black feminism, and the project of the rewriting of American
history, to include the full range of ethnic participation and experience.

In its capacity to find a basis for affirmation, Beloved is in marked
contrast to Don DeLillo's Mao II which also depicts cultures that seek
to obliterate naming and the life of the individual; without resort to
ideologies predicated on humanist progress, DeLillo's novel derives its
power and tone from representation of the grotesqueness of the familiar,
the numbness of the naturalised, and the desperation of the alienated.
There are few comforts or bolt holes outside of the considerable
pleasures of textuality.

From the studies here, decadence alone cannot be said to characterise
either writing at or about the ending of epochs. If the strength of the
grand narratives which fuelled Milton and Shakespeare's writing was

failing by the nineteenth century to the extent that notions of degeneration and decadence were in wide circulation in Europe, narratives of feminism, homosocial desire, and socialism which projected alternative, visionary futures may also be read in *fin de siecle* writing. Interestingly, none of the late twentieth-century work under discussion here is termed decadent. However, despite profound differences between the two periods, the twentieth-century range of response – fear, fascination, alienation, and vision – is similar to that found in writing of the 1890s.

Our anticipation of the millennium, our resistance to its trope of decay/decline, and our displacement of decadence by postmodernism can only be counted a partial success, postmodernism itself having been located within late capitalism and viewed as a decadent form. Within the grand narrative of Marxism, a system rooted in a customised and materialised biblical structure of apocalypse, judgement, and new life, the instrumental value of postmodernism in the ending of epochs and the prefiguring of a revisionist future indeed appears low. However, such disavowal of any single theory and the defence of eclecticism are precisely part of postmodernism's virtue, as well as its weakness. Liberation of writing from both the requirement to be 'great' and to be 'traditional' has freed up a huge amount and range of material.

The cumulative debates of poststructuralism and postmodernism have opened up English to texts of all registers including popular culture, renewed discussion of literary and cultural value, and facilitated serious consideration of literary politics. The tolerance and visibility of theory in Britain now is clearly one of the most remarkable outcomes of the transformation of English over the last twenty years. The other, stemming from an historical rather than formalist tradition, is the identification, visibility, and inclusion of countless authors occluded and excluded from re-publication and the canon by reason of gender, ethnicity, or sexual orientation. The virtual remapping of the history of literature in English has begun. In the rich cacophony of mid 1990s cultural discourse and texts, decadence is a strain, audible not dominant.

Laurel Brake
July, 1995

'Is this the end of this new glorious world?': 'Paradise Lost' and the beginning of the end

HELEN WILCOX

I

IF WE MUST CHOOSE somewhere to begin our consideration of 'the end' (the first but certainly not the last paradoxical thought in this essay) then there is no better era to focus upon than the seventeenth century in England. During its first decade actors performed, for the first time, Shakespeare's despairingly stark lines from the final scene of *King Lear*, when the aged Lear appears on the stage bearing the dead body of his dearest daughter Cordelia. Kent and Edgar, looking on aghast, ask in turn:

> Is this the promis'd end?
> Or image of that horror?   (5.3.262–3)

The play's tragic close, awful in itself, is given even greater powers of repercussion by Kent's words which evoke the ultimate 'promis'd end', the last scene of the drama of world history, the apocalypse. The sight of Lear in his agony of experience carrying the burden of destroyed innocence is, if not the apocalypse itself, then, in Edgar's phrase, an 'image of that horror'.

The image of the 'promis'd end' haunts the pages of seventeenth-century texts. In the early years of the century, Donne, too, was preoccupied with the drive towards the end of things, though in his case the image is created from a more personal perspective. In his 'Holy Sonnet' 7, Donne excitedly constructs the scene of the last day:

> At the round earths imagin'd corners, blow
> Your trumpets, Angells, and arise, arise
> From death, you numberlesse infinities
> Of soules, and to your scattred bodies goe,
> All whom the flood did, and fire shall o'erthrow,
> All whom warre, dearth, age, agues, tyrannies,
> Despaire, law, chance, hath slaine.

1

Here the end of the world, the final moment of history, is dynamically suggested in terms of the noise of the summons to judgement, the action of resurrection and the meeting of souls and bodies, and the almost unimaginable enormity of the event. However, the whole operation is suspended by Donne's individual intervention:

> But let them sleepe, Lord, and mee mourne a space,
> For, if above all these, my sinnes abound,
> 'Tis late to aske abundance of thy grace,
> When we are there;

Donne's angle is not cosmic but private; his animated vision of the Day of Judgement centres on the threat that judgement holds for him in particular. Despite being a poet of great beginnings, Donne was perpetually end-focussed; typically, in his first 'Holy Sonnet', he asks God to 'repaire' him urgently because 'mine end doth haste' – and with it, the first taste of judgement. As his last sermon, 'Death's Duell', repeatedly makes clear, human life is seen as a process of dying by degrees; to be mortal is to be marked by death even before birth, to begin the end before the beginning. But this perception is given most vivid embodiment in the voice of the poetic speaker who is approaching death itself:

> This is my playes last scene, here heavens appoint
> My pilgrimages last mile; and my race
> Idly, yet quickly runne, hath this last pace,
> My spans last inch, my minutes latest point,
> And gluttonous death, will instantly unjoynt
> My body, and soule, and I shall sleepe a space,
> But my'ever-waking part shall see that face,
> Whose feare already shakes my every joynt:
>
> ('Holy Sonnet' 6)

With a precise but dramatically imaginative intensity, Donne's speaker envisions not only his 'playes last scene' but also his 'pilgrimages last mile', the 'last pace' of his earthly 'race', his 'spans last inch' and 'minutes latest point'. Ending is fearful but almost endlessly, agonisingly, measurable in its inevitability. But death is deceptive; though it has the appearance of 'sleepe' and the body does indeed rest, there is one part which never sleeps, the 'ever-waking' soul, which must proceed to see the 'face' of God in expectation of judgement. Death may 'unjoynt' the body and soul, but even more to be feared is that which follows death and can shake 'every joynt' even in the anticipation.

The idea of the end, then, is a complex notion taking many forms in the seventeenth century. It is the tragic horror of human suffering which, as in the final scene of *Lear*, anticipates the apocalypse in its earth-shattering enormity. It is death itself, the end of an individual life and the 'last scene' of the personal human drama. But it is also the moment of final judgement which, though terrifying to Donne (and not only to Donne, of course), is simultaneously the triumphant conclusion of time, when the angels finally sound their trumpets at the 'round earths imagin'd corners'. In the harsh bright sound of the trumpet is expressed both threat and splendour; this is the music of battle but also of victory.

As the seventeenth century progressed, the end of things – in the full complexity of that notion – seemed to be getting very close. Unprecedented outbreaks of plague kept death always at hand. Scientists and theologians, as well as poets, anticipated the end of the world. Godfrey Goodman, for example, wrote at length in his *The Fall of Man, or the Corruption of Nature* (1616) about the degeneration of the creation and how everything in the world (except, perhaps, his own book) was shrinking in preparation for the imminent Last Judgement. If the world is in decline, the argument runs, this is all a part of God's plan and will lead eventually to the final universal conflagration. More and more individuals shared a sense that the events described in the Book of Revelation, such as the burning up of the natural world, were impending in England. Radical groups, including the Fifth Monarchists, were identified specifically by their millenarian beliefs, anticipating with joy rather than dread the signs of the end and the promised thousand-year rule of the saints. Marvell jokingly refers, in 'To His Coy Mistress', to the 'conversion of the Jews', another expected sign of the beginning of the end of the world:

> I would
> Love you ten years before the Flood:
> And you should, if you please, refuse
> Till the conversion of the Jews.
> My vegetable love should grow
> Vaster than Empires, and more slow.

Their love, he teasingly suggests, may span the whole of human history from Noah's flood to the final judgement, parameters which recall Donne's juxtaposition of 'all whom the flood did, and fire shall o'er-throw' in his 'Holy Sonnet' 7. But it is only a brief illusion to regard the conversion of the Jews – and therefore the Last Judgement which would follow that sign – as an event in the distant future, allowing the speaker plenty of time meanwhile to praise his 'Coy Mistress'. The whole elegantly flattering passage is prefaced by the provisional opening line, 'Had we but World enough, and Time', and the rest of the poem makes cruelly clear that there is certainly not enough world or time for such leisured loving. Time – both personal and cosmic – hurries on towards its end with the frightful speed of a 'winged charriot'. The apocalyptic allusion to the Jews is a reminder of how Marvell's verse, in its lighter as well as darker moods, is shot through with the sense of an ending.

The events of the Civil War intensified the apocalypticism of English writing. The end became something to long for, both as an escape from present suffering and as the hoped-for triumphant outcome of the struggle. In her 'Song composed in time of the Civill Warr', published in 1653, An Collins looks forward to the end of those times in which things were 'disjoynted by abuse'. (In this case, though the metaphor is strikingly similar to Donne's, the 'disjoynting' is public and national rather than the private and bodily 'unjoynting' in Donne's 'Holy Sonnet' 6.) Her vision of the future is an apt reminder that the end can be seen in glorious terms:

> The Sonns of strife their force must cease,
>   Having fulfild their crime,
> And then the Son of wished peace
>   Our Horizon will clime.

The dominant image of the apocalypse in the Book of Revelation is that to which Collins metaphorically refers – the description of Christ as 'one like unto the Son of man' coming 'with clouds', 'in his right hand seven stars: and out of his mouth went a sharp twoedged sword: and his countenance was as the sun shineth in his strength' (1.7–16). There is danger of judgement as well as defense from the 'twoedged sword', but this apocalyptic sight, which St John asserts 'every eye shall see' (1.7), is for An Collins the focus of her yearning during the Civil War. Her sense of an ending is based on faith rather than history:

> That there are such auspicious dayes
>   To come, we may not doubt,
> Because the Gospels splendant rayes
>   Must shine the World throughout:
> By Jewes the Faith shall be embrac't
>   The Man of Sin must fall,

> New Babell shall be quite defac't
>   With her devices all.

Collins's certainty that the gospel *'must* shine the World throughout' is at once a biblical imperative and a poet's rhetorical command. Similarly, the 'Babell' of mid-seventeenth century England *'shall* be quite defac't'. For Collins and her contemporaries the end was thus urgently desired. Their words, echoing those of Revelation, could inscribe an imminent future.

II

It is in this historical, biblical and literary context that we should place our consideration of Milton's *Paradise Lost*, the English epic of 'the end of this new glorious world'. Milton grew up in the century of end-consciousness that has been sketched so far. He participated centrally in the political events of the 1640s and 1650s, and wrote *Paradise Lost* out of the knowledge of millenarian hopes and the experience of bitter defeat. The end as reality as well as threat, as immediate loss and distant consolation, in fact the whole range of its meaning and impact, is to be found in Milton's epic.

But first things first! Is *Paradise Lost* not fundamentally a poem about beginnings rather than endings? Its most significant source is the first book of the Bible, Genesis, not the last book, the Revelation of St John. Its central characters are those credited with the origins of all that is important: God, the creator of 'all this world beheld so fair' (III 554); Adam and Eve, the first human creatures and 'our first parents' (IV 6); Satan, the first rebel 'hurled headlong flaming from the ethereal sky' (I 45), instigator of sin and death; and Christ, first-begotten Son of God, chief source of redemptive love and grace 'without end' (III 142). The major event of the epic is, as described in the opening line, 'man's first disobedience', and the poem's initial inspiration derives from Moses,

> That shepherd, who first taught the chosen seed,
> In the beginning how the heavens and earth
> Rose out of chaos   (I 8–10)

These lines are overwhelmingly focused on beginnings. Moses' action in teaching the Jews is, like Milton's epic, itself a 'first' and concerns the origins of the 'heavens and earth'. The phrase 'in the beginning' refers both to Moses' own era and to the beginning of the world which he describes. It also directly echoes the opening of the Bible, these being the first words of the first chapter of the Book of Genesis (and of St. John's Gospel) in the Authorised Version. Milton's brief account of the 'shepherd' Moses is thus crammed with a sense of origins and potential, not just by means of overt expression in 'first' and 'in the beginning' but also by the reference to 'chaos', being the primordial substance of creation, and 'seed', being the modest yet potent beginning of a living thing.

The profound irony of the story of our origins in Genesis and in *Paradise Lost*, however, is that it is the tale of the beginning of the end. The creation narrative is, by a fundamental paradox, perpetually linked with a narrative of loss, closure and death. The first independent human act swiftly ushers in the last, as the opening lines of *Paradise Lost* powerfully demonstrate:

> Of man's first disobedience, and the fruit
> Of that forbidden tree, whose mortal taste
> Brought death into the world, and all our woe,
> With loss of Eden   (I 1–4)

The tasting of the fruit by mortals is what makes them 'mortal'. From the moment of the fall, human life is, as Donne knew so well, a process of dying. Within three lines of the beginning of the poem the concern with origins has led directly to the ending of an epoch; the 'fruit' of paradise has become the consequence of sin; 'death' and 'woe' ensue and the timeless glory of creation shrinks into time-bound decay. Unlike so many of Milton's own lines, human existence is end-stopped.

Despite the enormity of the geographical and temporal space traversed by *Paradise Lost*, the most intensely felt loss in the poem is located in the narrower confines of the individual human being. On his first encounter with Eve after her 'rash hand' has plucked the forbidden fruit, Adam stares at her in 'horror chill' before exclaiming:

> O fairest of creation, last and best
> Of all God's works, creature in whom excelled
> Whatever can to sight or thought be formed,
> Holy, divine, good, amiable or sweet!
> How art thou lost, how on a sudden lost,
> Defaced, deflowered, and now to death devote?
>   (IX 896–901)

The first paradise lost here is the innocence of Eve, God's 'last, best gift' (V 19). She whose creation marked the end of God's creative bounty represents the beginning of fallenness. Eve's integrity and freedom are lost, and the dreadful impact of this is conveyed by Adam's need to repeat 'How . . . lost?' in line 900. In place of her devotion to God and to Adam the 'lost' Eve is 'now to death devote'. There is, as Eve in desperation later observes, 'no end but death' (X 1004). The definition of fallen humanity is 'man whom death must end' (X 797). Later Michael allows Adam a vision of the flood, and notes:

> How didst thou grieve then, Adam, to behold
> The end of all thy offspring, end so sad,
> Depopulation   (XI 754–6)

The 'sad' end here is not the apocalypse but the flood, associated by Donne and Marvell rather with the beginning than the conclusion of recorded history. But for Milton's Adam, looking ahead to the flood, what it signifies is the destruction for which he is responsible. The 'end' is the wasteful deaths of individuals and whole generations of his 'offspring'.

The individualising of loss within so comprehensive an epic is one of the most striking features of Milton's depiction of the sense of an ending in *Paradise Lost*. It is at the centre of a series of concentric circles, each in turn representing a broader sense of the end of things but each founded upon that original protestant humanist commitment to personal experience. The introduction of mortality into individual lives through the Fall is, in sequence, also suffered by the natural world:

> Earth felt the wound, and nature from her seat
> Sighing through all her works gave signs of woe,
> That all was lost.   (IX 782–4)

The perfect creation grows imperfect; the 'centric globe' becomes 'oblique' (X 671), and the familiar patterns of seasonal change mark the fallenness of nature:

> At that tasted fruit
> The sun, as from Thyestean banquet, turned
> His course intended; else how had the world
> Inhabited, though sinless, more than now,
> Avoided pinching cold and scorching heat?   (X 687–691)

Seeing this profound effect of the Fall on the once-perfect world around him, Adam laments:

> O miserable of happy! Is this the end
> Of this new glorious world, and me so late
> The glory of that glory, who now become
> Accurst of blessed, hide me from the face
> Of God, whom to behold was then my highth
> Of happiness: yet well, if here would end
> The misery, I deserved it, and would bear
> My own deservings; but this will not serve;
> All that I eat or drink, or shall beget,
> Is propagated curse.   (X 720–729)

Milton's use of the word 'end' in this passage, each time poised significantly at the end of a line, highlights the inequality of endings in human experience. The miserable Adam perceives that the 'new glorious world' is altered, even brought to an 'end', by his actions. However, the consequent human 'misery' will, ironically, be without an 'end', being spread and 'propagated' through his descendants. The gloom and judgement of an eschatological outlook are, paradoxically, endless.

The loss of the Edenic paradise, the direct consequence of the 'evil hour' of the Fall, is itself an image of the end of the wider world at the apocalypse. Adam's question, 'Is this the end / Of this new glorious world?', echoes Kent's cry at the close of King Lear: 'Is this the promis'd end?' The absence of the word 'promis'd' in Adam's perplexed enquiry simply reminds us that at this point he has not yet seen a vision of the future, nor could he have read the Book of Revelation where the 'promise' is written. However, to emphasise the parallel between the end of the smaller world of Eden and the anticipated end of the whole world, Milton as poet seeks the prophetic voice of Revelation in order to warn Adam and Eve of the impending events:

> O for that warning voice, which he who saw
> The Apocalypse, heard cry in heaven aloud,
> Then when the dragon, put to second rout,
> Came furious down to be revenged on men,
> *Woe to the inhabitants on earth!* that now,
> While time was, our first parents had been warned
> The coming of their secret foe, and scaped
> Haply so scaped his mortal snare;   (IV 1–8)

Here Milton reminds his readers of the direct parallel between the first
battle in heaven and descent of Satan (the 'secret foe' who is about to
enter Eden) and the second battle between Michael and the dragon as
described in Revelation (12.7–12) where the dragon, too, 'came furious
down'. While Satan's threatening presence signifies the impending end
of Adam and Eve's paradisal world, the dragon's appearance is an
expected sign of the last days of the larger world. This is Milton's only
naming of the Apocalypse in *Paradise Lost*, and the conjunction of
prelapsarian and contemporary time in the words 'that now, / While
time was' (IV 5–6, above) is fascinating. The reference to 'now' has an
immediacy which appears to be at odds with the following phrase and
its past tense 'time was'. This is not simply an account of 'then' but also
an appeal to 'now'. Adam and Eve did not know then that their world
was about to end. Milton's readers, on the other hand, would have been
alert to the sense of urgency and the echo of Revelation 12.12: 'he
knoweth that he hath but a short time'. Milton's preoccupation with
the end of things does not simply have an historical focus; it has
prophetic impact, too.

III

There is, therefore, a range of 'ends' and concepts of 'ending' to be
encountered in *Paradise Lost*. These include individual human mortality, the loss of paradise itself and its anticipatory parallels with the end
of the whole world. All of these notions of ending are also shadows of
the expected end of the poetic narrative itself, to which attention will
be given before the end of this paper. However, it is important in the
meantime to consider to what extent the end has merely negative
connotations in Milton's epic. So far it has appeared, in its many
varieties, to be overwhelmingly undesired, since it signifies death, loss
and destruction. Those things which are beautiful or perfect are described approvingly as 'without end' – Christ's love (III 142), for
example, or the 'wondrous' God (V 165), and the world beyond time
is celebrated in terms of 'Eternity, whose end no eye can reach' (XII
556). Thus the very idea of ending would seem to be a feature and
consequence of the fall: an unwanted human necessity rather than a
divine wish.

There are, however, many uses of the word 'end' and its associated
ideas in *Paradise Lost* which have more positive implications. These
uses can betray another postlapsarian element; that is, the idea of the

end as relief from the suffering initiated by the fall. Thus, 'torture *without* end' (I 67), for example, is not a desirable state but a definition of utter misery. In such contexts the idea of finiteness is a relative good in a sorrowful world. But there are further, more genuinely positive contexts for the notion of the end, the most significant of which is the idea of the fortunate fall. Had the 'new glorious world' not come to an 'end' (X 720–1) through the original sin of Adam and Eve, then the greater good, the redemptive generosity of Christ, would not have been called upon:

> O goodness infinite, goodness immense!
> That all this good of evil shall produce,
> And evil turn to good; more wonderful
> Than that which by creation first brought forth
> Light out of darkness!   (XII 469–73)

Out of the end of paradise comes 'goodness infinite' – goodness without an end – a wonder paralleled with the beginning of creation though claimed as greater still. And this is the 'happy end' (XII 605) referred to in Michael's last words in the epic. By meditation upon this positive sense of ending, Adam is to sustain himself in the years outside Eden. For, as we are assured by Milton earlier in the poem, God himself is both the 'Author and end of all things' (VII 591). The parallel drawn in book XII between the 'happy end' and the first act of creation is no accident, for in a providential universe all things, including both the beginning and the end, are centred in God.

The idea of the end as located in, and in fact synonymous with, God himself – yet another dimension to the Miltonic concept of ending – must remind us that the noun 'end' means not only conclusion but also purpose. It is in this sense, too, that God is the 'end': the ultimate destination *and* guiding principle of human life. Michael warns Adam to remember that he is created 'to nobler end / Holy and pure, conformity divine'. In this usage, the end is not a postlapsarian necessity but the will which drives created life. The unfallen Adam undertakes to

> observe
> Immutably [God's] sovereign will, the end
> Of what we are   (VII 78–80)

while the serpent Satan is condemned because he was 'polluted from the end / Of his creation' (X 167). The end here is both reason and justification. Created things are defined by their purpose, the point (in rationality as well as in place and time) towards which they are destined. The fallen angels' fruitless discourse of 'providence, foreknowledge, will and fate' is doomed to hopelessness: they 'found no end, in wandering mazes lost' (II 559, 561). For once Milton places the word 'end' in the middle, and not at the end, of a line, and the reason is clear. The end is lost in the midst of confusion. The lack of end, in the sense both of purpose and of conclusion, is the key characteristic of sinfulness. Without an 'end' one wanders, or errs, in the 'maze' of experience.

Thus it would be wrong to suggest that the idea of the end is necessarily negative in *Paradise Lost*. In the complex web of pre- and postlapsarian perceptions which make up the epic, the end signifies motivation and mortality, loss and redemption, human weakness and divine essence. Most significantly, it is not so much contrasted with the idea of beginning as paralleled with it by Milton. The interconnected-ness of first and last, of beginning and end, is stressed from the opening lines of the poem as we saw earlier. The 'first disobedience' brought about the ultimate obedience of human life to a mortal end in death. When Satan arrives in paradise Milton describes that 'happy seat of man' as the fiend's 'journey's end and our beginning woe' (III 632–3), irrevocably joining not only Satan's purpose and the coming fall but also the very concepts of ending and beginning. Even in the brief and passing phrase 'prime end', used by Adam (VIII 540) with reference to the aim of nature in Eve, Milton again paradoxically combines the first or primary with the last or ultimate purpose. And at the beginning of the last book of the epic the archangel Michael sums up what has gone before with a concise statement uniting the creation and the fall: 'Thus hast thou seen one world begin and end' (XII 6).

IV

How, then, does Milton manage to end his own poem, this epic which abides by no laws of chronology and is generically boundless in its material and perspective? There is no plain progress from beginning to end. Rather, as the opening lines of the poem evoke endings, so the closing lines are concerned with beginnings. Once Michael has con-cluded his speech to Adam by urging him to meditate on the 'paradise within' (XII 587), that redemptive 'happy end' (XII 605) brought about by Christ, the poem confronts new beginnings with sober optimism. The last word is given to Eve, who has learnt through a dream that from her womb will stem the line of daughters leading ultimately to Mary, and thus in her final line she can assert that 'By me the promised seed shall all restore' (XII 623). Her closing words are not like those of Kent in *King Lear* with their expectation of the 'promis'd end'. On the contrary, what Eve's vision promises is a 'seed', in this case the precious life of Christ and thus the beginning of new life for all.

There are further hints of newness and beginnings in the closing lines of *Paradise Lost*. The direction in which 'our lingering parents' depart from paradise is towards the east. They are led out of Eden by the 'eastern gate' (XII 638), the aspect of the garden to be associated with the dawning of a new day, as well as with the crucifixion when, as Donne concisely expressed it, 'a Sunne, by rising set' would 'by that setting endlesse day beget' ('Goodfriday, 1613'). Most memorably, the epic faces a new world in its final few lines as Adam and Eve choose their new 'place of rest': 'The world was all before them' (XII 647, 646). Weeping 'some natural tears' at their loss of paradise, the first human couple move tentatively towards a new beginning. As the poem closes,

> They hand in hand with wandering steps and slow,
> Through Eden took their solitary way.   (XII 648–9)

The poem ends on the threshold of newness, the beginning of the rest of human history. The echo of the lines describing the fallen angels' 'wandering' thoughts (II 561) is intriguing. Were Adam and Eve, too, denied the possibility of finding an 'end'?

This raises the question of the ultimate impossibility of ending. Milton's poem indeed comes to an end – after the lines just quoted, the rest is silence – but its pattern of thought, metaphor and argument all insist upon continuation and renewal. Even in one of its most apocalyptic moments, facing up to the time beyond the end of the poem when the end of the world will come, *Paradise Lost* foresees not the end but newness and eternity:

> thy saviour and thy Lord,
> Last in the clouds from heaven to be revealed
> In glory of the Father, to dissolve
> Satan with his perverted world, then raise
> From the conflagrant mass, purged and refined,
> New heavens, new earth, ages of endless date
> Founded in righteousness and peace and love
> To bring forth fruits joy and eternal bliss.   (XII 544–551)

The only end here is the dissolution of the 'perverted world' of the devil. All the emphasis otherwise is on revelation, restoration, re-creation and an 'endless' future. The forbidden fruit has given way to the 'fruits of righteousness' (Philippians 1.11), just as the fallen world will be replaced by a 'new heaven and a new earth' (Revelation 21.1). Perhaps it is the impossibility of imagining a world which has ceased to exist – a task even more demanding than reconstructing the beginning of the world from nothing – that leads to the profoundly forward-looking conclusion of both *Paradise Lost* and the Bible. Even the Book of Revelation, which concludes the Bible, finishes not with the end but with a hopeful expectancy: 'Even so, come, Lord Jesus' (22.20). So it should come as no surprise, perhaps, that Milton finds complete closure at the end of *Paradise Lost* both impossible and inappropriate.

Despite the linearity of recorded time and written words, despite even the sense of decay, the threat of mortality and the promise of the Last Things, the residual mode of human thinking is cyclical. In individual terms this takes the form of returning to that from which we came. As Milton puts it, once again merging beginning and end, birth and death, 'we end / In dust, our final rest and native home' (X 1084–5). In terms of human redemption the cycle is expressed in Christ, the 'Alpha and Omega, the beginning and the ending' (Revelation 1.8) who, in his person, unites the first and last and thus turns the sequential line of the alphabet and of time into a circle. So when Adam asks, 'Is this the end / Of this new glorious world?' (X 720–21), the answer has to be that even while the 'new glorious world' is ending, the next new world, in this case the inner paradise of redeemed humanity, is beginning. An absolute end is, if not unimaginable, at least inexpressible within the bounds of the epic. The conclusion of Pope's *Dunciad* comes close to achieving it, but even there the real blackout comes after the last line of the poem. Milton ends much less apocalyptically than Pope, with adherence instead to a redemptive cycle which brings rebirth and renewal. A closer parallel may be found in Herbert's 'Church', his sequence of devotional lyrics which begins with 'The Altar' and ends with the heavenly banquet of 'Love' (III). The pattern of progress would appear to be from the earthly place of worship to the joys of eternity. However, the first poem represents a 'broken altar', an imperfect celebration, and by the end of the final poem the speaker is at last ready to resume the incomplete eucharist of the first: to 'sit and eat' once more. The pattern is one of progression but also of returning and starting again. The cyclical experience of the poems in Herbert's sequence brings the reader to the beginning once more.

Bearing in mind this parallel with the devotional circularity of Herbert's 'Church', it becomes evident that it is not only possible but also quite in keeping with its doctrines and history that *Paradise Lost* should be both a tragic epic of the beginning as end and a triumphant assertion of the end as beginning. This paradoxical conclusion may be summed up in a phrase of Adam's to Michael just before the end of the poem, uttered when Adam has heard of the life of Christ which is to come. Michael, and by implication Christ, is addressed by Adam as 'finisher / Of utmost hope!' (XII 375–6). Once again, Milton deliberately places a word concerned with the end – 'finisher' – at the end of the line, and in the description as a whole the ambiguity of ending is itself highlighted. The 'finisher' is the one who reaches the end, in this case bringing redemption, which is identified here with the final or 'utmost hope'. But the poem has also been largely concerned with the processes of the fall, through which Satan finished off human hopes of paradise. He, too, is evoked in the shadows of Milton's phrase as one who was in a more negative sense the 'finisher' of the aspirations of humankind. The contradictory meanings of 'finisher' as both completer and destroyer epitomise the paradoxes of *Paradise Lost* and the idea of ending.

How should a discussion of endings end? Following Milton's example, the most appropriate mode of conclusion would be a new beginning to complete the cycle of creation, fall and rebirth – which, to a certain extent, is no ending at all. But as an interim end, at least, where better to pause than with Adam's lines to Raphael urging him to continue his narrative of the mysteries of creation:

> Or if the star of evening and the moon
> Haste to thy audience, night with her will bring
> Silence, and sleep listening to thee will watch,
> Or we can bid his absence, till thy song
> End, and dismiss thee ere the morning shine.   (VII 104–8)

In the midst of his epic, Milton contemplates, through the words of Adam, how both to extend and to end the 'song' of Raphael, which is a mirror of his own. And for the first time, the word 'end' appears at the beginning of a line, triumphantly preceding the dawning of a new day.

Works Cited

Collins, An, 1653. *Divine Songs and Meditations*, London.

Donne, John, 1985. *Complete English Poems*, ed. C.A. Patrides, London: Dent.

Goodman, Godfrey, 1616. *The Fall of Man, or the Corruption of Nature*, London.

Herbert, George, 1974. *Complete English Poems*, ed. C.A. Patrides, London: Dent.

Marvell, Andrew, 1984. *Complete Poetry*, ed. George deF. Lord, London: Dent.

Milton, John, 1971. *Paradise Lost*, ed. Alastair Fowler, London: Longman.

Shakespeare, William, 1974. *King Lear*, ed. Kenneth Muir, London: Methuen.

Shakespeare and the End of History

GORDON McMULLAN

I

THE STUDY OF a writer's late work as often as not invokes two apparently incompatible models of history, linear and cyclical. The concept of the career (with one possible OED definition humorously quoted by Michael Millgate as 'a short gallop at full speed') seems to imply a conscious, if imperilled, linearity, within which 'late writing' can be seen either as evidence of decline or as an act of will, a looking forward beyond death, a bequeathing, a rejection of the finality of the final (Millgate 1992, 2). At the same time, this bequeathing can be, and often is, manipulative, a deliberate rewriting of the past for the benefit of posterity. In this sense, the 'testamentary act' can be seen as cyclical rather than linear, a return to the 'early' in order to reshape it for those coming after. In other words, late writing is as much about revision, rethinking, and reshaping for the future as it is about finality.

The peculiar tensions and uncertainties that characterise Shakespeare and Fletcher's *Henry VIII* are, I would argue, the product of its status as just such a 'testamentary act.'[1] Coming as it does at the very end of Shakespeare's career, the play has been seen as a failure or at best a partial success, as evidence of artistic decay or actual illness. Even those who accept that the play is collaborative tend to read the partnership with Fletcher as a possible sign of weakness or lack of interest, begrudging Shakespeare his return to professional activity in the wake of *The Tempest*. Yet it is also possible to see the play's disjunctions as deliberate, and to argue that, in turning back to history thirteen years after *Henry V*, Shakespeare is knowingly returning with experimental motivation to a form associated with the early part of his career in a manner characteristic of the 'testamentary act.'

In his work on late nineteenth-century writers, Michael Millgate notes alternative etymologies for the term 'testament.' Two in particular

---

[1] The evidence for *Henry VIII* as a joint composition by Shakespeare and Fletcher seems to me to be conclusive. See, in particular, Hoy 1962. For a useful recent contribution to the debate, see Hope 1994.

16

hold resonances which are curiously apposite for analysis of *Henry VIII*. The word, he observes,

> has popularly taken on something of the aura of its now archaic meaning of 'covenant,' especially as found in scriptural accounts of the Last Supper (according to the Authorized version). Its use in legal contexts may also have tenuously attracted to it the sense of testifying or bearing witness, the word 'testator,' indeed, having historically been used as meaning both 'one who makes a will' and 'one who or that which testifies; a witness'. (Millgate 1992, 186)

The religious significance of 'testament' has immediate relevance for a play which looks back to the time of England's break with Rome and which examines the meaning of the birth of Elizabeth for English history. The play's religious (or perhaps better, ecclesiological) meditations, though, remain unsettling, exploring issues of conscience and motivation at the time of the Henrician schism whilst avoiding representing that schism directly. This evasion of direct representation is itself typical since it is the question of 'testimony,' of pinpointing and recounting the truth, which is repeatedly at stake in the play's uncertainties. The act of witnessing is demonstrated to be essential to the construction of history, and it is history as construct, rather than as event, which is emphasised throughout.

I would argue that an examination of the logic of truth in *Henry VIII* suggests that the play is best viewed as a complex and unsettling meditation on the 'end of history,' simultaneously promoting and denying the possibility of truth at a moment of cultural crisis within which the word 'Truth' held very specific sectarian resonances. In deploying the phrase 'the end of history,' I wish to invoke both eschatology and historiography: on the one hand, the sixteenth and seventeenth century apocalypticism (the End of History) that provided a radical symbolic base for Protestants in their political and aesthetic struggle with the counter-reformation, and on the other, the late twentieth century acknowledgment of the radical textuality of historical representation (the 'end of history'), a recognition whose roots lie in the development of the writing of history – and of 'history plays' – in the early modern period. *Henry VIII* is thus, I would argue, in several senses a 'testamentary act': it is a 'late work' which explores the possibilities and problems of testimony and truth in order to examine the contemporary status of an historical covenant.

II

The word 'truth' turns up no fewer than twenty-five times in *Henry VIII*, along with eighteen appearances of 'true' (nineteen, if you count the title of the play as reported by contemporary observers, *All is True*), six of 'truly,' and one of 'true-hearted.' The Prologue alone offers two mentions of 'truth' and one of 'true,' connecting the concept first of all with a nexus of faith, hope and expenditure ['Such as give/Their money out of hope they may believe,/May here find truth' (Prologue 7–9)], then with a sense of deliberate selectivity or, perhaps, election ['our chosen truth' (Prologue 18)], and finally with the relationship between artistic intention and representation ['the opinion that we bring/To make that only true we now intend' (Prologue 20–21)].[2] The play seems almost to tease its audience with 'truth,' hinting at contemporary relevance while retaining a certain ambivalence: 'Think ye see/The very persons of our noble story/As they were living' (Prologue 25–7), the Prologue demands, though it is not clear whether this is merely an exhortation to forget the time-lapse between the events on stage and the England of the present, or whether it is a broad hint that the characters have their counterparts in contemporary politics. A number of recent critics have opted for the latter, reading the emphasis on 'truth' as a straightforward assertion of the conscious topicality of the play.

The year of first performance of *Henry VIII* was an extraordinary one for English politics and in particular for the politics of English Protestantism. The death of Henry, Prince of Wales, in November 1612 shattered the millenarian hopes that militant Protestants had invested in him, with his passion for military display and his allegiance to the dream of a Protestant Europe. Henry's enthusiasm for the impending marriage of his sister Elizabeth to Frederick the Elector Palatine, the principal Continental Protestant ruler, was taken up with a fervour verging on desperation after his death, with the result that (ostensibly, at least) James and his militant Protestant subjects were in atypical harmony at the beginning of 1613. Henry's death had been a terrible blow, though, and the outpouring of grief for the dead prince was continually in danger of overshadowing the celebrations for the wedding, which was postponed to February. Like its sister collaboration *The Two Noble Kinsmen*, *Henry VIII* dwells on the mixed negative and

---

[2] All references to *Henry VIII* are to Foakes 1957 and will be given parenthetically in the text.

positive emotions induced by the rapid succession of funeral and
wedding.[3] The Prologue predicts a melancholy play: 'if you can be merry
then, I'll say/A man may weep upon his wedding day' (Prologue 31–2).
And the two wry choric Gentlemen, commenting on the speed of
political and emotional change, capture (as they do throughout the
play) the mood of the moment:

> 2 Gent.   At our last encounter
> The Duke of Buckingham came from his trial.
> 1 Gent.   'Tis very true. But that time offer'd sorrow,
> This general joy.   (IV. i. 4–7)

It is hard not to see a parallel between the emotions expressed on stage
at moments such as this and the political situation at the time of
composition. And it is not surprising that those critics who concentrate
on the topicality of the play are also most closely concerned with its
relationship to Protestantism.

R.A. Foakes, in his influential Arden edition, points out that a 'play
on the downfall of Wolsey, the last great Catholic statesman of England,
on the rise of Cranmer, and the birth of 'that now triumphant Saint
our late Queene Elizabeth' would have been very appropriate at such a
time' (Foakes 1957, xxxi).[4] He suggests that Henry VIII may well have
been performed for the wedding itself, demonstrating a series of verbal
parallels between contemporary descriptions of the occasion and the
unusually detailed stage-directions in the Folio text, and emphasising
the deliberate parallels drawn between Princess Elizabeth and her
earlier namesake in sermons and pamphlets at the time. Frances Yates,
in Shakespeare's Last Plays, examines the political effect that nostalgia
for Elizabeth exercised in James's reign and notes the focus of Protestant
hopes on Prince Henry. For her, Henry VIII is an unequivocally Protestant play which 'reflects the Foxian apocalyptic view of English
history' (Yates 1975, 70).[5] More recently, William Baillie has analysed

---

[3] The Two Noble Kinsmen arguably echoes the prevailing emotions of 1613
by way of its unique tragicomic conclusion (a wedding and a funeral, simultaneously), voiced most succinctly by Palamon: 'That we should things desire
which do cost us/The loss of our desire! That naught could buy/Dear love but
loss of dear love.' See Waith 1989, V. iv. 110–112.
[4] Julia Gasper, though, disagrees, pointing out that to perform a play 'largely
concerned with divorce . . . at a royal wedding would surely have been an
offence against taste and decorum' (Gasper 1993, 207).
[5] Wickham 1993, however, finds a very different aim, arguing that the play

a series of topical motifs in the play which would be of particular relevance to militant Protestants, including 'the expansion of the monarch's personal authority in relation to the law, the sudden fall of a court favorite, and a divorce' (that of the Earl of Essex and Frances Howard) (Baillie 1979, 248). And Donna Hamilton has extended these claims, the latter in particular, arguing that *Henry VIII* aims specifically to discredit the 'Howard faction at court – a faction dominated by Catholics – by associating their values and projects . . . with Wolsey and the values he represents' (Hamilton 1992, 164). The consensus of these views (whatever the flaws of some of the individual arguments) is that *Henry VIII* was involved to a substantial degree in the politics of Protestantism at the time of composition.

'Topical' critics tend to emphasise the very last scene of the play – and in particular Cranmer's prophecy over the child Elizabeth – to support the general principle that *Henry VIII* celebrates and projects a future for English Protestantism under James. Yet curiously, despite the rigorous contextualisation effected by these readings, there is a further broad context which has yet to be acknowledged in topical readings of *Henry VIII*, but which is crucial for any reading which aims to assess the play's claims about truth. For Cranmer's language in the last scene and the many other references to truth in the play belong to an established tradition of sectarian appropriation which has clear associations with the crisis of 1612–13. 'Let me speak sir,' Cranmer demands of the king, 'For heaven now bids me; and the words I utter,/Let none think flattery, for they'll find 'em truth' (V. iv. 14–16). The child Elizabeth, he claims, 'promises/Upon this land a thousand thousand blessings,/Which time shall bring to ripeness' (18–21). In this time of revelation, he tells us,

> Truth shall nurse her,
> Holy and heavenly thoughts still counsel her;
> She shall be lov'd and fear'd: her own shall bless her;
> Her foes shake like a field of beaten corn,
> And hang their heads with sorrow. . . .
> God shall be truly known, and those about her
> From her shall read the perfect ways of honour.
>
> (V. iv. 28–32, 36–7)

was designed to rehabilitate Katherine of Aragon, presumably to pave the way for Catholic matches in the future.

'Truth Liberated by Time': Woodcut from William Marshall's *Goodly Prymer in Englyshe*, 1535 (Saxl 1936.205).

And he goes on to foreshadow James's reign after the 'maiden phoenix' (40) has been called by heaven 'from this cloud of darkness' (44):

> Peace, plenty, love, truth, terror,
> That were the servants to this chosen infant,
> Shall then be his, and like a vine grow to him;
> Wherever the bright sun of heaven shall shine,
> His honour and the greatness of his name
> Shall be, and make new nations.   (V. iv. 47–52)

This repetition of 'truth,' particularly in the context of revelation, read in tandem with the emphasis on Elizabeth's election, invokes the resurgence in 1612–13 of a sectarian iconography which had developed around the concept in the course of the previous century.

The appropriation of 'Truth' for Protestant iconography has been traced as early as 1521, when John Knoblouch of Strasbourg, printer to a range of advocates of religious reform from Erasmus to Luther, had deliberately used as his printer's mark an image of Truth personified as a harassed woman emerging from a cave (Saxl 1936; see also Chew 1947, Fabiny 1984). The belligerently anti-Catholic use to which Knoblouch's image was in due course put in England is clear from the titlepage woodcut to William Marshall's *Goodly Prymer in Englyshe*, published shortly after the Henrician schism, in which medieval images of the Harrowing of Hell are reworked to depict 'the liberation of Christian Truth (as seen by Protestant reformers) from her captivity under the monster of Roman hypocrisy' (Saxl 1936, 203). The introduction here of the figure of Time as Truth's rescuer forcefully appropriates the motto *Veritas Filia Temporis* ('Truth the daughter of Time'), which focusses on the temporal revelation of Truth in the framework of apocalypse. Truth was claimed by both sides in the course of the sixteenth century, acquired for Edward VI, reappropriated for Roman Catholicism by Queen Mary at her accession, and then revived by Elizabeth for Reformed religion (Chew 1947, 69–70). Shortly after she came to the throne, Elizabeth went on a procession through London and was greeted by a figure representing Time leading a white-clad Truth who handed to Elizabeth the *verbum veritatis*, the Bible in English (Chew 1947, 70–71). Keen to confirm her association with Truth, the queen allegedly stopped and cried out, 'And Time hath brought me hither!'

It is this specifically Elizabethan appropriation, best known from the figure of Una in Book One of Spenser's *Faerie Queene*, that is key to the

resurgence of the iconography of Truth at the time of the first production of *Henry VIII*. The playwright Thomas Dekker had forcefully
dramatised the associations of the Time-Truth image early in James's
reign in *The Whore of Babylon*, which Gasper calls 'the definitive
militant Protestant play' (Gasper 1990, 62). As the play opens, Truth
awaits the death of Mary so that she and her father Time can help
Elizabeth (in the shape of Titania, the Fairy Queen) defeat the malign
forces of the Whore of Babylon. The printers of the 1607 Quarto
incorporate marginal glosses to help the reader negotiate the significance of the allegory, but by 1612 such interpretative assistance would
have been unnecessary. Two examples of entertainments heavily invested with the iconography of *Veritas Filia Temporis* will serve to
demonstrate the status of Truth at the time of Prince Henry's death: the
anonymous *Masque of Truth* and Thomas Middleton's *The Triumphs of
Truth*.

Middleton's entertainment was the first of his series of six pageants
written for mayors of London in the 1610s and 1620s. *The Triumphs of
Truth* was, according to David Norbrook, the most expensive of all such
pageants in the Renaissance: 'for no other state occasion in James's
reign did the City summon up so much enthusiasm' (94). It echoes the
typology of Spenser and Dekker, presenting a 'lengthy struggle . . .
between a female figure representing Truth', who is 'poor, thin, and
threadbare,' and 'idolatrous Error' (94) riding in a glorious chariot. The
arrival of Time precipitates an apocalyptic scene '[a]t which a flame
shoots from the head of Zeal, which fastening upon that chariot of Error,
sets it on fire, and all the beasts that are joined to it,' so that, by the
close of the pageant, with the help of a few fiery special effects, the
'proud seat of Error' lies 'glowing in embers,' and Truth is triumphant.
Middleton here seeks ways to instigate a 'reformation of the masque,'
to reform a genre associated by English Protestants with James's unmili-
tant tendencies: the pageant draws on the Protestant triumphalism
revived by the wedding of Elizabeth and Frederick after the shock of
the death of Prince Henry, and as such is designed to send a strong
message from city to court at a time of sectarian crisis.

It seems that Henry's death had already caused an iconographic
reversal in the midst of the wedding celebrations themselves, a dilution
of the Protestant fervour Henry had championed in the aesthetic arena,
since there is evidence of an overtly apocalyptic masque-project for the
wedding – *The Masque of Truth* – which was promoted by Henry but
aborted immediately after his death (Norbrook 1986). The cancellation of this masque is of particular note because, where Middleton's

pageant serves as an address to the court from outside, *The Masque of Truth* seems to have been initiated and supported from within. In the event, it was replaced by a conservative masque commissioned from Thomas Campion, a client of the Howard family, who (as Hamilton's analysis shows) were decidedly at odds with militant Protestant aspirations (Campion 1967; Hamilton 1992; McMullan 1994). No original text of *The Masque of Truth* is extant, but we do have an outline and partial transcription in French, which makes its apocalyptic allegiances abundantly clear. As the masque begins (or would have begun), Atlas is tired of holding up the world, and has come to England to give up his 'burden to Aletheia (Truth), . . . represented on stage by a huge reclining statue reading a Bible and holding a globe in her left hand' (Norbrook 1986, 83). The Muses call on the various nations of Europe 'to pay tribute to King James for his patronage of the Truth' (Norbrook 1986, 83). Europe and her five daughters – France, Spain, Germany, Italy, and Greece – then bow to Truth and offer tribute to James. At the very end of the masque, 'the globe splits in two and disappears, leaving behind it a paradise guarded by an angel bearing a flaming sword' (Norbrook 1986, 83). Truth invites the various nations to repent and enter paradise, and the gates close behind them.

'Truth' can be seen in this context to be a highly loaded term, a Protestant absolute implying a militant foreign and domestic politics and with a heavy investment in the cult of Henry, Prince of Wales. As a result, the project offers a very different view of the marriage of Elizabeth and Frederick from that promoted by James. It presents the union not as the first of a series of Protestant and Catholic marriages designed to bring Europe together in peace but as a 'confessional alliance': James, as guardian of English Calvinist Protestantism, by uniting with the Protestant Palatinate, will ensure that the other nations bow to Reformed religion. It is clear enough why the masque was never performed: it would not exactly have been a diplomatic coup. But if Prince Henry did have a hand in its design, then its cancellation in the immediate wake of his death underlines the immensity of his loss to English militant Protestants.

III

This context for Truth would seem to confirm readings of *Henry VIII, or All is True* as a firmly Protestant, apocalyptic play. Cranmer's prophetic emphasis on Time and Truth evokes an iconographic tradition central to the representation of Protestant hopes and it provides a resounding resolution to the political dilemmas dramatised in the course of the play. Yet several critics (e.g. Bliss 1975) have rejected readings of *Henry VIII* which begin with Cranmer's speech and then look back at previous events in light of that speech. For these critics, there is a strangeness, an uncertainty, about *Henry VIII* which is not resolved by locating the play within a tradition of unquestioning apocalypticism: Cranmer's prophecy may come as a final revelation in the play and it may seem to echo the language of apocalypse, but (*pace* Frances Yates) *Henry VIII* can hardly be called an apocalyptic play. As Clifford Leech pointed out nearly forty years ago,

> Of all the last plays [*Henry VIII*] is the one that most clearly indicates the cyclic process. Nothing is finally decided here, the pattern of future events being foreshadowed as essentially a repetition of what is here presented. (Leech 1958, 29)

Paul Dean similarly suggests that in *Henry VIII* there is no 'organic and cumulative movement toward a single concluding point' (Dean 1986, 178). And for Frank Cespedes, the play, despite its status as a 'history play,'

> annuls eschatology and teleology. Against the optimistic principle of providential history invoked by Cranmer, the play emphasises the uncertainties of history in order to question the availability of an 'omniscient' perspective on historical events.
>
> (Cespedes 1980, 416–7)

This suggests a tension (a defining tension, even) within *Henry VIII* between linear and cyclical forces. It is as if the play sets the Protestant teleological vision against a mythic sense of time as a cycle; and the key issue provoked by this linear/cyclical struggle becomes, perhaps oddly, not structure but tone. After all, while apocalypticism is typically humourless, the cyclical and the ridiculous are rarely far apart: the inevitable repeat and return of serious events makes them more ironic, less serious.

Juxtaposing two examples of testimony – a description within the play of an event prior to the action of the play and a contemporary eyewitness description of a performance of *Henry VIII* – might help to underline the nature of the play's uncertainties. The testimony from the play proper is Norfolk's description of the Field of the Cloth of Gold (I. i. 13–38); the account of the performance is the letter of Henry

Wotton which is the principal evidence for the date of first production. Critics seem to agree that the opening scene is in many ways representative of the play as a whole 'in its insistence on the second-hand nature of our acquaintance with historical events' (Dean 1986, 182). It is, as Gasper puts it, 'an artful piece of time-release poetry ... which appears to be a panegyric of the court, but which reveals more and more scepticism, disgust and ridicule the more often we read it' (Gasper 1993, 208). Initially, though, we take Norfolk's glorious description at face value. He describes himself to Buckingham as 'ever since a fresh admirer' (I. i. 3) of the spectacle put on by the kings of England and France as they met to conclude peace at the Field of the Cloth of Gold:

> To-day the French,
> All clinquant all in gold, like heathen gods
> Shone down the English; and to-morrow they
> Made Britain India: every man that stood
> Show'd like a mine. . . . Now this masque
> Was cried incomparable; and th'ensuing night
> Made it a fool and beggar. The two kings
> Equal in lustre, were now best, now worst,
> As presence did present them: him in eye
> Still him in praise, and being present both,
> 'Twas said they saw but one, and no discerner
> Durst wag his tongue in censure.   (I. i. 18–22, 26–33)

Yet within a few dozen lines we gather that the whole thing was a waste of time, a temporary peace which 'not values/The cost that did conclude it' (I. i. 88–9). And we recognise, looking back at the speech, that it expressed a kind of relativism. The English and French are each viewed in light of the other, with no firm ground for judgement: 'The two kings/Equal in lustre, were now best, now worst,/As presence did present them' (I. i. 28–30). And we are brought up sharp with recognition of the emptiness of the grand gesture. As Lee Bliss observes, in arguably the best reading of *Henry VIII* to date, '[i]n the beginning all had seemed true to Norfolk and, in his report, to us; only in retrospect can we see how false, how truly unstable . . . that appearance was' (Bliss 1975, 3). And we rapidly come to the conclusion that

'admire' did not signify wonder in the sense of approbation, but rather an ironic sense of amazement at the disparity between a dream of transcendent and transforming harmony and the disconcertingly mutable political realities of an impoverished nobility and a broken treaty. (Bliss 1975, 3)

In Norfolk's testimony, then, judgement and therefore truth are seen to be at best contingent. The accolade goes to the champion of the moment, but the decision is arbitrary, the moment fleeting, and the triumph glitteringly hollow.

Sir Henry Wotton's letter describing one of the first performances of the play implies in a different way that grandeur is by definition short-lived. Pomp cannot withstand scrutiny, since familiarity breeds contempt:

> The King's players had a new play, called *All is true*, representing some principal pieces of the reign of Henry VIII, which was set forth with many extraordinary circumstances of pomp and majesty, even to the matting of the stage; the Knights of the Order, with their Georges and garters, the Guards with their embroidered coats, and the like: sufficient in truth within a while to make greatness very familiar, if not ridiculous. (Smith 1907, 32–3)

Wotton is clearly concerned that pomp without distance becomes revealing and therefore self-defeating. The truth (i.e. the irony) of the accuracy and care with which the play represents royal ceremony seems akin to Toby's efforts in *Tristram Shandy* to explain where he was wounded: the more precisely you show the details, the further from the truth you move and the more ridiculous you seem. In *Henry VIII* this movement is most clearly embodied in the conversations of the two choric Gentlemen, notably in Act IV, as they watch the Coronation procession pass by.

The detailed stage directions in the First Folio are echoed in the Gentlemen's comments:

> 2 Gent. A royal train, believe me: these I know;
> Who's that that bears the sceptre?
> 1 Gent.   Marquess Dorset,
> And that the Earl of Surrey with the rod.   (IV i. 37–39)

This detailing is apparently neutral: we simply absorb the display of power without question. Until, that is, the Gentlemen begin to move towards their more usual mode of irony. We have already seen the way in which conscience and lust have become intertwined in the king's manoeuvrings to gain Anne Bullen. The king repeatedly claims it is his

conscience about his technically incestuous relationship with
Katherine that is driving him to divorce. But the audience's suspicions
of his motivations are compounded by his turn of phrase when he speaks
of his regret at leaving 'so sweet a bedfellow,' crying 'But conscience,
conscience;/O 'tis a tender place, and I must leave her' (II. ii. 142–3).[6]
Shortly afterwards, in mocking Anne for disguising ambition within
her ostensible modesty, the Old Lady speaks with heavy innuendo of
'the capacity' of Anne's 'soft cheveril conscience' to receive gifts, if she
'might please to stretch it' (II. iii. 31–3). These moments of irony
resurface at Anne's coronation. The Second Gentleman seems wholly
caught up in the ceremony, but his rhapsody concludes with a suggestive, and politically dangerous, bathos:

> Our king has all the Indies in his arms
> And more, and richer, when he strains that lady;
> I cannot blame his conscience   (IV. i. 45–7)

His friend ignores this aside, but returns to the topic himself a few lines
later. 'These are stars indeed – ' says the Second Gentleman, admiring
the courtly women, to which the First Gentleman adds, 'And sometimes falling ones,' a remark risqué enough (laying bare, as it does,
Anne's perceived route to power) to produce a 'No more of that' from
his interlocutor. Detail, then, both of the king's motivations and of the
practical staging of royal display, leads directly to ridicule, greatness
made thoroughly over-familiar.

The issue of testimony thus foregrounds the uncertainties of the play.
There is no firm basis for the interpretation of events: witnessing and
irony become blood-brothers. And it is not just interpretation but
events themselves which seem ever more problematic as the play goes
on. For Pierre Sahel,

> [m]ost of the events of Henry VIII are echoed – more or less unfaith-
> fully – within the play itself. They are not dramatized but reported
> after having passed through distorting filters. Characters present
> incidents and occurrences – or, often, their own versions of incidents
> and occurrences. (Sahel 1985, 145)

---

[6] As Judith Anderson and others have pointed out, the phrase 'tender place'
is at best ambivalent at this moment. See Anderson 1984, 128–9; also
Rudnytsky 1991, 51.

The effect of this filtering of events is to sustain a sense of radical uncertainty throughout the play. For Sahel, it is rumour which sets the tone: rumour sometimes as a political tool, sometimes simply as the 'buzzing' (II. i. 148) which seems constantly to be going on in the background of each scene. Despite fears of suppression ['no discerner/Durst wag his tongue in censure' (I. i. 32–3)], rumour is never silenced. The absolute Truth upon which the Prologue seemed to stand and upon which Cranmer's prophecy will depend is rapidly submerged in report and opinion.

The relationship between rumour and truth is overtly questioned at the beginning of Act II in another of the Gentlemen's conversations. '[D]id you not,' asks the Second Gentleman, 'of late days hear/A buzzing of a separation/Between the king and Katherine?' 'Yes,' replies his friend,

> but it held not
> For when the king once heard it, out of anger
> He sent command to the lord mayor straight
> To stop the rumour, and allay those tongues
> That durst disperse it.

To which the Second Gentleman immediately retorts:

> But that slander, sir,
> Is found a truth now; for it grows again
> Fresher than e'er it was, and held for certain
> The king will venture at it.   (II. i. 147–156)

That clause 'held for certain' neatly captures the tone: certainty occupies the same space as opinion. Truth, in this context, is equated with slander: the two seem interchangeable, dependent simply upon the succession of events and the way things are viewed from moment to moment. Communication thus becomes a process which simultaneously transmits and degrades truth, an organic and inescapable infection: 'it grows again/Fresher than e'er it was.' The build-up to this exchange of rumour is both revealing and complex. The Second Gentleman drops a broad hint of occult knowledge: 'yet I can give you inkling/Of an ensuing evil, if it fall,/Greater than this' (II. i. 140–2). His friend's eager, staccato reply is a masterpiece of contradiction, desiring while denying the desire to know the truth (or, rather, the rumour). It also emphasises faith, not just as trustworthiness but as

belief: 'Good angels keep it from us:/What may it be? you do not doubt
my faith sir?' To which the Second Gentleman responds, teasingly,
'This secret is so weighty, 'twill require/A strong faith to conceal it.'
'Let me have it,' cries the First Gentleman, 'I do not talk much,' a
comment generally guaranteed to raise a laugh in performance, since
the only capacity in which we have seen the speaker is as a gossip and
rumour-monger.

Faith and truth are thus contiguous, and they are equally abused in
the process of communication. In fact, the play seems to move towards
a proleptic acknowledgement of current definitions of testimony. For
Shoshana Felman and Dori Laub, testimony is

> not simply (as we commonly perceive it) the observing, the record-
> ing, the remembering of an event, but an utterly unique and irre-
> placeable topographical *position* with respect to an occurrence.
>   (Felman and Laub 1992, 206)

Individual testimony becomes not one person's perspective on a single
coherent truth of which the witness sees only one facet, but rather 'the
uniqueness of the *performance of a story* which is constituted by the fact
that, like the oath, it cannot be carried out by anybody else' (Felman
and Laub 1992, 206). Certainly, *Henry VIII* seems to dwell on the
radical and unbridgeable difference between the perspectives different
witnesses have on the same event, to the extent that the event itself
cannot clearly be said to have happened. Far from sustaining a sense of
Truth as a Protestant absolute, the play makes truth an impossibility.
Everyone, from Buckingham and his surveyor to Wolsey and Cranmer,
claims a monopoly of truth. They cannot all be right. This is the
fundamental problem for any attempt to locate the play's obsession with
truth in relation to apocalyptic, militant Protestantism, and it puts
intolerable pressure on the last scene. The key question is whether this
equivocal mood can be fully transformed by Cranmer's prophecy,
whether apocalyptic Truth can assert herself above the arbitrariness of
the rumour-ridden political world, and even whether the prophecy is
as resolutely apocalyptic as has been claimed.

IV

There is little doubt that, for all the problems of truth and testimony
the audience have witnessed by the time they arrive at Elizabeth's
christening, Cranmer's prophecy nonetheless has a powerful and direct

emotive charge. Foakes is clearly right in arguing that the Jacobean audience would have been attuned to two Elizabeths and two royal ceremonies. The prophecy is thus directed at a series of futures, some already completed by 1613, others still projected. And it depends heavily upon the audience's hindsight for its success. The completed predictions serve to validate those as yet unfulfilled, offering a clear linear dynamic to the eschatological mindset, but it is important both to recognise the play's rejection of direct historical agency and to ponder the expected response to the unproven predictions, in particular the Jacobean audience's reading of the scene's references to and predic-tions for King James. And I would argue that the play demands the deployment of hindsight as a means to examine the contemporary status of the Reformation in England.

Part of the curiosity of Cranmer's speech is that it seems to ascribe to James imperial aspirations which were associated with militant Protestantism but which were at best marginal to the king's own preferred policies. Apocalypse and Empire have a traditional intimacy: here it is the colonisation of America, promoted by Protestants but viewed with suspicion by the king, which is emphasised in 'predicting' James's achievements ['Wherever the bright sun of heaven shall shine,/His honour and the greatness of his name/Shall be, and make new nations' (V. iv. 50–52)].[7] Moreover, the 'phoenix' metaphor by which Cranmer fudges James's relationship to Elizabeth is shared with that most militant of Protestant plays, Dekker's Whore of Babylon:

> [O]ut of her ashes may
> A second Phoenix rise, of larger wing,
> Of stronger talent, of more dreadfull beake,
> Who swooping through the ayre, may with his beating
> So well commaund the winds, that all those trees
> Where sit birds of our hatching (now fled thither)
> Will tremble, . . . yea and perhaps his talent
> May be so bonie and so large of gripe,
> That it may shake all Babilon.   (Dekker 1607, F2ᵛ)

James, however, had little intention of shaking 'all Babilon': his interest was in establishing Continent-wide peace by way of dynastic marriage and in confirming his personal appropriation of the seventh beatitude, Beati Pacifici. And of course juxtaposing Cranmer's prophecy with the

---

[7] On Apocalypse and Empire, see Kermode 1967, 10ff.

passage from Dekker simply serves to underline the relative bloodless-
ness of Cranmer's 'apocalyptic' vision. More to the point, as Julia
Gasper observes, it is noticeable that though Cranmer makes several
biblical allusions in the course of his prophecy, he refers each time to
Old Testament prophets and resolutely avoids the obvious text for
apocalyptic visions, the Book of Revelation (Gasper 1990, 97). The
relationship between Cranmer's prophecy and Protestant apocalypticism thus begins to seem very uncomfortable, particularly when seen
in the particular 1612–13 context. And I would argue that it becomes
still more problematic with the recognition that the christening scene
invokes powerful visual as well as verbal images, drawing on two
separate iconographic traditions, each of which presents Henry VIII in
a less than flattering light. The first is the tradition of *Veritas Filia
Temporis* which we have already examined as a broad context for the
play's obsession with Truth; the second is the iconography of David and
Bathsheba.

It is important to remember that, in the christening scene, it is
Archbishop Cranmer, not King Henry, who occupies centre stage along
with the infant Elizabeth. He stands over the child to make his
climactic prophecy, and at this key moment of celebration, the scene,
I would argue, evokes in a very specific way the iconography of *Veritas
Filia Temporis*. The effect of this evocation is to exclude the king from
the sacramental scene: at the precise moment in which Elizabeth
inherits the mantle of English Protestantism, she is presented to the
audience as the spiritual, if not the natural, daughter of Cranmer rather
than of Henry. As we have already noted, the language of the prophecy
encourages us to see the future Queen Elizabeth as the incarnation of
Protestant Truth ['Which time shall bring to ripeness' (V. iv. 20)], and
if, as Judith Doolin Spikes has suggested, the figure of Time in *The
Whore of Babylon* informs the portrayal of Cranmer here in *Henry VIII*,
then this is confirmed by the iconography (Spikes 1977, 140). With
Henry to one side, amazed by the archbishop's words, the audience sees
the familiar vignette: Time stands over Truth and rapturously predicts
the End of History. The moment serves abruptly to decentre the king,
removing him from full paternity and leaving the circumstances of
Elizabeth's birth (and consequently her legitimacy) as shrouded as her
death in Cranmer's prophecy.

I would thus argue that an iconographic interpretation of this moment, taken together with the ambivalence of the portrayal of the king
throughout, rejects the Erastian readings sometimes made of the play,
rigorously questioning Henry's spiritual authority and thus by

implication (extrapolating from the equation of Queen Elizabeth and Princess Elizabeth noted by Foakes) that of King James. Moreover, a second, more covert layer of iconographic potential at the moment of Elizabeth's christening can be seen to exacerbate the discomfort of this moment for James. The reference to 'Saba' (the Queen of Sheba) in Cranmer's prophecy obliquely associates the young Elizabeth with David's son Solomon, implying her adoption of Solomon's various attributes (notably that of wisdom). But seen in conjunction with the sidelining of King Henry and the absence of Anne Bullen at this key moment of the play, it also offers an additional, politically unsettling possibility.

The story of David's desire for and adultery with Bathsheba, his arrangement for the death in battle of her husband Uriah, and his subsequent repentance following denunciation by Nathan the prophet was one of the best-known of Old Testament stories, and an iconographic tradition had grown up which associated David's 'Penitential Psalms' with the Bathsheba story, particularly the initial image of David watching Bathsheba bathing.[8] Reformation readings of 2 Samuel 11–12 tended to emphasise the story as an example of the inevitability of sin and the necessity of repentance, partly in reaction to a Roman Catholic tradition of fairly breathtaking licence in which David's desire for Bathsheba was interpreted as Christ's desire for his Church, Uriah became the 'Prince of this World,' and David's adultery was conveniently reworked as his rescue of the Church from the Devil (Réau 1956, 273–77; Zim 1987, 70; Tyndale 1528, 135^v–136^r). Certainly, the Penitential Psalms, like the image of *Veritas Filia Temporis*, were well-known as a Reformation battleground and were associated with the development of Protestant doctrine (Greenblatt 1980, 115, 276). The story had, though, been given a dark political significance during the reign of Henry VIII by Sir Thomas Wyatt, who produced verse-translations of the Penitential Psalms, was rumoured to have had an affair with Anne Boleyn before the king met her, and was imprisoned by the king at the time of her execution.[9] According to Rivkah Zim, Wyatt 'may have seen King David – the royal lover guilty of manslaughter, if not

[8] The 'penitential psalms' are a traditional grouping of Psalms 6, 32, 38, 51, 102, 130 and 143. On the iconography, see Ewbank 1965, 3–40; Zim 1987, 70–74; Parkes 1979, 175, plate 88; Fisher 1509, aa^{2}r. I am grateful to Professor Richard Proudfoot for suggesting the relevance of the David and Bathsheba story for the study of *Henry VIII*.

[9] For the poetry of Thomas Wyatt, see Rebholz 1978.

murder, in the pursuit of illicit passion – as representing Henry VIII'
(Zim 1987, 73–4; also Greenblatt 1980, 115, 146–7). It would be hard
to deny the dangerous resonances the story held for King Henry,
desperately awaiting the birth of a son. David's penitence is such that
God lets him live, but his punishment is the death of his first child by
Bathsheba. The conception and birth of Solomon in the wake of this
marks the return of God's favour, and is confirmed by an alternative
name for the child, Jedidiah, 'beloved of God,' given him through
Nathan the prophet.

It is thus possible to read the last scene of *Henry VIII* through an
alternative iconographic tradition which associates the birth of Elizabeth
and her subsequent life and reign with the return of God's favour to his
chosen nation in the wake of sinful and adulterous behaviour on the
part of the king. Cranmer's centrality as the counterpart of Nathan the
prophet has the effect once more of marginalising King Henry in his
uncomfortable equivalence to the easily-tempted David, God's
anointed, but not always entirely reliable, king. And this might well
have uneasy resonances for 1612–13, particularly if the audience were
again to see in the character of Henry VIII a shadowing of King James.
In view of Dennis Kay's assertion that the death of Henry, Prince of
Wales, was widely represented, in a kind of nationwide act of penitence,
as 'divine retribution for the nation's sin' (Kay 1990, 134), an awkward,
and presumably highly dangerous, topical interpretation is on offer. The
iconographic retreat from Erastianism we have already registered is thus
highly telling. The English Reformation is represented at the climactic
moment of the play both as something which has happened and as
something which is still to happen, even in the reign of James I.

The last scene thus exemplifies the inherent contradictions of the
play. In a practical exposition of the Derridean idea that truth is
produced at the moment of the dissolution of truth, it is possible to see
that the iconographic triumph of Protestant propaganda is achieved at
a moment which highlights the contemporary uncertainties of the
claim. The scene is a looking-forward to the future which is also a return
to the past, mythologising the transition from Elizabeth to James by
way of the (unhistorically direct) transition from Henry to Elizabeth,
and at the same time strongly hinting at the ambiguous status of the
militant Protestant apocalyptic project under James. *Henry VIII* can
thus be seen as a meditation on the state of the English Reformation
in 1612–13 which sets linear and cyclical models of history against each
other in order to project a future for English Protestantism which is at
the same time a return to the past.

V

There is one further level on which *Henry VIII* can be seen as a testamentary act, a very specific act of 'will.' Marking and, I would argue, embracing the transition from Shakespeare to Fletcher (the scene of Cranmer's prophecy is, after all, Fletcher's, not Shakespeare's), *Henry VIII* returns to Elizabeth and to the history play both to mark the genre's roots in Shakespeare's early work and to project its future in Fletcher's post-Shakespearean plays. For Shakespeare to give up this moment to Fletcher (whose usual pattern of collaborative work was to write the central acts of a play and leave the beginnings and endings to his partner) can be read not as a sign of weariness or illness but as a significant gesture, an apparent selflessness which is in fact a projection of self. It is a gesture which looks forward to an ideal future, to a new reign which will be both different and the same, even as it recognises that successors rarely live up to their predecessors' hopes. In other words, Shakespeare's *not* writing the scene of Cranmer's prophecy can in itself be regarded as a testamentary act, disabling all readings of the play which view the scene as a culmination, a conclusion. It is no more final than any of the other episodes that have made up the play. To project a future, it returns to the past, a progression at once linear and cyclical, sustaining the hegemony both of Shakespeare and of the King's company, succession assured. As a memorial to the ending of epochs, *Henry VIII* can thus be seen as both a testamentary act and a self-consuming artifact.

Works cited

Anderson, Judith H., 1984. *Biographical Truth: The Representation of Historical Persons in Tudor-Stuart Writing*, New Haven: Yale UP.

Baillie, William, 1979. '*Henry VIII*: a Jacobean history,' *Shakespeare Studies* 12, 247–266.

Bliss, Lee, 1975. 'The wheel of fortune and the maiden phoenix in Shakespeare's *King Henry the Eighth*,' *English Literary History* 42, 1–25.

Campion, Thomas, 1967. *The Lords' Masque*, ed. I. A. Shapiro, in *A Book of Masques in Honour of Allardyce Nicoll*, Cambridge: Cambridge UP, 95–123.

Cespedes, Frank V., 1980. ' "We are one in fortunes": the sense of history in *Henry VIII*,' *English Literary Renaissance* 10, 413–38.

Chew, Samuel C., 1947. *The Virtues Reconciled: An Iconographic Study*, Toronto: U of Toronto P.

Dean, Paul, 1986. 'Dramatic mode and historical vision in *Henry VIII*,' *Shakespeare Quarterly* 37, 175–189.

Dekker, Thomas, 1607. *The Whore of Babylon*, London.

Ewbank, Inga-Stina, 1965. 'The House of David in Renaissance Drama: A Comparative Study,' *Renaissance Drama* 8, 3–40.

Fabiny, Tibor, 1984. '*Veritas filia temporis*: the iconography of Time and Truth and Shakespeare,' *Acta Universitatis Szegediensis de Attila Jozsef Nominatae: Papers in English and American Studies* 3, 215–271.

Felman, Shoshana, and Dori Laub, 1992. *Testimony: Crises of Witnessing in Literature, Psychoanalysis, and History*, New York: Routledge.

Fisher, John, 1509. *Treatyse concernynge the fruytfull saynges of Davyd the kynge and prophete in the seven penytencyall psalmes*, London.

Foakes, R.A., 1957. William Shakespeare [and John Fletcher], 1957. *King Henry VIII*, ed. R.A. Foakes, London: Methuen.

Gasper, Julia, 1990. *The Dragon and the Dove: The Plays of Thomas Dekker*, Oxford: Clarendon P.

Gasper, Julia, 1993. 'The Reformation plays on the public stage,' in J.R. Mulryne and Margaret Shewring (eds), *Theatre and Government under the Early Stuarts*, Cambridge: Cambridge UP, 190–216.

Greenblatt, Stephen, 1980. *Renaissance Self-Fashioning: From More to Shakespeare*, Chicago: U of Chicago P.

Hamilton, Donna, 1992. *Shakespeare and the Politics of Protestant England*, Hemel Hempstead: Harvester.

Hope, Jonathan, 1994. *The Authorship of Shakespeare's Plays: a socio-linguistic study*, Cambridge: Cambridge UP.

Hoy, Cyrus, 1962. 'The shares of Fletcher and his collaborators in the Beaumont and Fletcher canon, VII,' *Studies in Bibliography* 15, 71–90.

Kay, Dennis, 1990. *Melodious Tears: The English Funeral Elegy from Spenser to Milton*, Oxford: Clarendon P.

Kermode, Frank, 1967. *The Sense of an Ending*, Oxford: Oxford UP.

Leech, Clifford, 1958. 'The structure of the last plays,' *Shakespeare Survey* 11, 19–30.

McMullan, Gordon, 1994. *The Politics of Unease in the Plays of John Fletcher*, Amherst: U of Massachusetts P, 1994.

Millgate, Michael, 1992. *Testamentary Acts: Browning, Tennyson, James, Hardy*, Oxford: Clarendon P.

Norbrook, David, 1986. ' "The Masque of Truth": court entertainments and international Protestant politics in the early Stuart period,' *The Seventeenth Century* 1, 81–110.

Parkes, M. B., 1979. *The Medieval manuscripts of Keble College, Oxford*, London: Scolar P.

Réau, Louis, 1956. *Iconographie de l'art chrétien*, vol. II, Paris: Presses Universitaires de France.

Rebholz, R. A., 1978. Sir Thomas Wyatt, *Collected Poems*, ed. R. A. Rebholz, Harmondsworth: Penguin.

Rudnytsky, Peter L., 1991. '*Henry VIII* and the deconstruction of history,' *Shakespeare Survey* 43, 43–58.

Sahel, Pierre, 1985. 'The strangeness of a dramatic style: rumour in *Henry VIII*,' *Shakespeare Survey* 38, 146–8.

Saxl, Fritz, 1936. 'Veritas Filia Temporis,' in R. Klibansky and H. J. Paton (eds), *Philosophy and History: Essays Presented to Ernst Cassirer*, Oxford: Oxford UP, 197–222.

Smith, Logan Pearsall (ed.), 1907. *The Life and Letters of Sir Henry Wotton*, 2 vols, Oxford: Clarendon P.

Spikes, Judith Doolin, 1977. 'The Jacobean history play and the myth of the Elect Nation,' *Renaissance Drama* 8, 117–149.

Tyndale, William, 1528. *The obedience of a Christen man and how Christen rulers ought to governe*, Antwerp.

Waith, Eugene, 1989. William Shakespeare and John Fletcher, *The Two Noble Kinsmen*, ed. Eugene Waith, Oxford: Oxford UP.

Wickham, Glynne, 1993. 'The dramatic structure of Shakespeare's *King Henry the Eighth*: an essay in rehabilitation,' in *British Academy Shakespeare Lectures, 1980–89*, introduced by E.A.J. Honigmann, Oxford: Oxford UP for the British Academy, 117–136.

Yates, Frances, 1975. *Shakespeare's Last Plays: A New Approach*, London: RKP.

Zim, Rivkah, 1987. *English Metrical Psalms: Poetry as Praise and Prayer, 1535–1601*, Cambridge: Cambridge UP.

Endgames:
The Politics of The Yellow Book or, Decadence, Gender and the New Journalism

LAUREL BRAKE

I. Gender

'in the age we live in one gets lost among the genders'
(H. James, 'The Death of the Lion,' YB 1, 1894, 44)

THE NOTION OF gender, re-introduced into general discourse in the late 1960s by the revived feminist critique of culture, has come to characterise our episteme, just as surely as tropes of revolution, democracy, class, capital, and Culture produced and inhabited discourses from other epistemes. If the last decades of the nineteenth century were always already perceived as decadent by older salvationists such as Arnold and Ruskin, younger contemporaries such as Yeats and Nordau supplied epithets – 'tragic' and 'degeneration' – which resonate in our own estimates a century later. Elaine Showalter's approach to the cultural matrix of these decades as years of 'sexual anarchy' at once conflates the apocalyptic teleology of millennarianism, in which anarchy is positive and purgative with the anti-democratic politics appropriated by Arnold, who based the maintenance of 'culture' and civic order on the obliteration of anarchic elements. However, as rereadings emerge from critics/readers writing self-consciously within the category of gender, the reinscriptions of Victorian writing 'find', *throughout* the century, a preoccupation of discourse with gender, from the Wordsworths, the Carlyles, and Tennyson and Hallam onward.[1] Schoolboys, bachelors, friends, cads, lovers, protectors, guardians, adventurers, heroes, dandies, husbands, rakes, lechers, authors, and narrators are alike reinscribed in gendered spaces, as are schoolgirls, friends, companions, heroines, intellectuals, new, fallen, and independent women, wives, dependants, aunts, spinsters, mothers, sisters, gossips,

---

[1] See for example, Dellamora 1990, Poovey 1988, Tuchman 1989, Walkowitz 1992.

governesses, seamstresses, and activists. Whereas the latter decades of the nineteenth century had been seen as outstanding for their 'decadence,' a critique of gender categories and sexuality in discourse (which the nineteenth-century apothegm 'decadence' both hints at and occludes) was, it now 'appears,' manifesting itself throughout the period.

In the 'takes' on the subject of gendered discourse in the 1890s periodical press that follow, I frame the periodical rather than authors or single articles. At moments the frame narrows to focus on articles, or widens to include other debates about and within gendered discourse in other periodicals, and in related cultural formations such as the book trade, and the publishing and newspaper industries. I want to move discussion of these periodicals from the backroom of apparently apolitical discourse about aestheticised, 'decadent', self-referring exotica into proximity with the gendered discourse and sexual politics of more general contemporary periodicals and books. These include *The Fortnightly Review, The Humanitarian, The New Review, The Artist and Journal of Home Culture, The Westminster Review,* and *The Westminster Gazette.* My comparisons suggest that although *The Yellow Book* and its offspring *The Savoy* distinguished themselves from many other serials of their day through their apparent exclusion of politics in favour of a proclaimed focus on literature and visual art, their 'aesthetic' discourses of naturalism, symbolism, nihilism, erotica, and graphics cohabit with insistent discourses of gender, with sexual as well as cultural politics.

The Savoy is comprised of a range of aggressively male and in the main heterosexual discourses, with the notable exception of Beardsley's contributions. *The Yellow Book,* despite its deployment of Ella d'Arcy in an editorial capacity and its regular contributions by women, is so suffused with male discourses of gender, in work by women and men, that these male discourses characterise the journal as much as its 'aestheticism.' Two pieces in Vol. I, the homage to the prostitute in Arthur Symons' poem 'Stella Maris' and Ella d'Arcy's vituperative portrait of an 'irremediable' marriage between a vacuous working-class bride and her despairing middle-class husband, suggest the parameters of such discourses. Part of the politics ostensibly disavowed in the name of disinterestedness in the Prospectus, *The Yellow Book's* diverse and often metaphysical discourses of gender largely avoid the sensual voyeurism prevalent in *The Savoy* with its comparative preponderance of male contributors.[2] Readers in both the nineteenth century and our

---

[2] For *The Savoy* see Stokes 1989 and 1990, and '*The Savoy*: 1896. Gender in Crisis?' in Brake 1994, 148–65.

own have identified and reacted to the 'sex' in *The Yellow Book*, but whereas in the 1890s the issue was its presence, its constructions occupy twentieth-century analysts.

This particular moment in the discourses of gender, of *The Yellow Book* and *The Savoy*, is bifurcated and determined by the trials of Oscar Wilde, themselves the occasion for articulation of a great range of address to issues of gender. But while the barely established *Yellow Book*, a year old, 'turned grey overnight' in April 1895 after it purged Beardsley, and although the brief life of *The Savoy* (January–December 1896) resulted from this purge, neither periodical ever published or even mentioned Wilde or the trials. Nor did they explicitly link their own inscriptions of gender (for example, Henry Harland's 'A Responsibility' (YB II) – a sad tale of failed male bonding – which appeared before the trials) with the discourses of homophobia and homosexuality revealed and provoked by the widely reported trials. However 'avant-garde' these magazines are, and however permeated with gender inscriptions, they articulate too the homophobia of their period, and indicate the extent of anxiety attaching to gender as a subject and the delimitations of its discourses.

Scrutiny of the wider periodical press in the 1890s brings into view other cultural formations and discourses which pertain to gender in the aesthetic press. Within journalism these include the literary formation of male novelists who blame women readers and writers, and institutions they associate with them (such as the circulating libraries) for the constraints on English fiction, and who wish to reclaim the novel from such women; the social purity campaign, fired by the work of Josephine Butler and W.T. Stead; women writers, feminist and non-feminist; writers whose base is science, comprising Darwinists, sexologists, psychologists, and behind them medical discourse; publishers and publishing, of both books and serials; journalism, journalists, and the 'new journalism'; and the 'new [homosexual] culture' which takes in practitioners of literature, visual art, and criticism.

These formations are overwhelmingly male, some exclusively. Women are in the main perceived as 'other,' even within formations which include them such as journalism: it inscribes them, for example, as '**women** journalists.' To set beside the discourses of *The Yellow Book* and *The Savoy*, I want to move into view the Society of Women Journalists in 1895–6 which was chaired by John Oliver Hobbes [Mrs Craigie], a contributor to *The Yellow Book*; journalism by women; and the existence in the 1890s of a range of women's newspapers. In November 1894, during the short heyday of *The Yellow Book*, the

Fortnightly Review, edited then by Frank Harris, ran an article on 'Women's Newspapers' which lists and discusses an array of titles, and concludes that Britain's weekly women's press is unique in its diversity, generality of coverage, and capacity for seriousness:

> Whatever be their shortcoming, there are no women's papers the least like these in any other country. Those which have a wide circulation in America are sensible and useful, with a strong religious tone, but are principally calculated for young girls, and compare on more equal terms with the *Girl's Own Paper* or the *Young Woman* . . . those published in Australia and New Zealand are of the same kind, but not so good. There are excellent French and German domestic papers, confining themselves purely to dress and housewifery, and recognising little change in women's views. All bring out suffrage papers, but these are confined to a small circle, and the majority of those of general interest published in other countries are really extremely poor. It may be, and has been said, that it is a mistake for women to sever themselves from men, thereby setting up a different standard; and we are told that Frenchwomen, for example, avoid the danger. No doubt the intellectual woman will habitually turn for her news to the ordinary papers, but the diverse subjects with which she is now specially connected in this country, demand a fuller treatment than the ordinary paper will give them. For instance, when the Women Workers' Conference takes place in the autumn, an event of deep interest to hundreds, if not thousands, of women, the general papers scarcely touch upon it. (March Phillipps 1894, 669)

Phillipps' argument that the 'ordinary [male] paper' cannot be relied upon by women for full coverage of women-related *news* has a dimension only implicit in the *Fortnightly*: while this progressive monthly addresses the woman question, it cannot be relied upon by new women readers to support basic elements of the cause. This may be seen in the *Fortnightly*'s practice in 1894: if in November it published March Phillipps' celebratory piece on women's newspapers and journalists in Britain, earlier, in March, it had carried an article on 'The New Hedonism'[3] by Grant Allen, author of an 1889 *Fortnightly* piece, 'Plain Words on the Woman Question', which had defined women overwhelmingly in terms of their biology; the March '94 article and the

---

[3] Allen is alluding to Wilde who used this phrase and developed the idea in *The Picture of Dorian Gray* in 1891 (Wilde 1981, 22); Murray notes Wilde's debt in this passage to Pater's 'Conclusion' (Wilde 1981, 226).

debate that it stimulated in the press between August and October affords us a view of positions on gender to parallel those in the 'decadent' press.

The New Hedonism

In many respects the arguments of Allen's 'The New Hedonism' can be seen to harmonise with the reputation of *The Fortnightly*, as edited by Frank Harris, for publication of advanced and progressive views, typified by Harris's publication of Wilde's aphorisms 'The Soul of Man Under Socialism' and 'A Preface to *Dorian Gray*' in February and March 1891. Allen's defence of the 'new hedonism' is presented as an attack on asceticism and theology; flamboyantly libertine, it is couched in an advocacy of beauty and of 'self-development' rather than 'self-sacrifice,' which calls to mind both Walter Pater's 'Conclusion' to *The Renaissance* and its corrective the 'new Cyrenaism' of *Marius the Epicurean*, together with its outgrowth the 'new culture' of homosexuality with which the undergraduate magazine *The Spirit Lamp* allied itself in 1893 under the editorship of Alfred Douglas. The depiction of the unstinting pursuit of self-development recommended by Allen is modelled palpably on Pater's 'Conclusion', and the rhetoric of aestheticism is appropriated:

> And what is thus true of the body corporeal is true also of the body spiritual, intellectual, aesthetic. It is the duty of everyone among us to develop himself and herself to the highest possible point, freely, in every direction. It is our duty to think as far as we can think; to get rid of all dogmas, preconceptions, and prejudices; to make sure we are not tied by false fears or vague terrors; to examine all faiths, all fancies, all shibboleths, political, religious, social, moral. . . . It is our duty to search and probe into all these things; taking nothing for granted, accepting nothing on authority, testing all we are told by teacher or preacher, by priest or savant, by moralist or schoolmaster. We should each of us arrive at a consistent theory of the universe for ourselves, and of our own place in it. (Allen 1894, 381)[4]

---

[4] Allen's last sentence here is distinct from Pater's position in the 'Conclusion' where he rejects all theories, metaphysics, and consistency, advocating instead a sturdy empiricism which adjusts to the exigencies of the moments.

So too with culture. Every unit of gain in the aesthetic sense, every diffusion of a wide taste for poetry, for art, for music, for decoration, is to the good for humanity. (Allen 1894, 382)

Allen's rationalist, secularist address to 'the sexual relation' as an explicit subject in the remainder of the article chimes with its centrality in the contemporary *Yellow Book* and *Savoy*: 'everything high and ennobling in our nature springs directly out of the sexual instinct. . . . To it we owe the entire existence of aesthetic sense, which is, in the last resort, a secondary sexual attribute' (Allen 1894, 384). It is a measure of difference from the conditions in which Pater's oblique if suggestive final paragraphs from the 'Conclusion,' first appeared twenty-five years before, in an anonymous review of another's work which the reviewer's positions in the conclusion appeared to arise from.

A second element significantly distinguishes Allen's 'The New Hedonism' from Pater's 'Conclusion' and much of the contents of *The Yellow Book* and *The Savoy*: its commitment to a heterosexuality linked with social purity, which emerges over time and in the main retrospectively, in what was presented as a serialised extension of the original article as an authorial reply in the ensuing debate. 'About the New Hedonism' appeared in September in another periodical, *The Humanitarian. A Monthly Review of Sociological Science*, a shilling monthly publication of the Humanitarian League, edited by Victoria Woodhull (1838–1927), journalist, orator and suffragist. In 1890 Woodhull had co-authored a book with her sister called *The Human Body: The Temple of God*, and as a younger journalist in the U.S. she was imprisoned with her sister for obscenity pertaining to an article on Henry Ward Beecher's alleged double life. While *The Humanitarian* (1892–1901) like *The Fortnightly* was prepared to publish a range of views, it seems from this 'New Hedonism' sample that the grounding of *The Humanitarian* in gender politics freed the two contributors outside the dominant discourse – the secularist 'social purity'/sexologist, and the gay man – to be more explicit in the articulation of their views than the mainstream *Fortnightly* or the chary, eclectic *Yellow Book* could permit. Allen's disclosure of his social purity position which accords with one strand of feminism (cf. Sarah Grand) may be thought to suit the political space in which it appears, but his explicit rejection of homosexual love seems gratuitous; social purity does not demand such a ban (see Grand's *Heavenly Twins*) and *The Humanitarian* publishes a defence of Greek love as part of the New Hedonism debate. Certainly, the second tranche of Allen's New Hedonism manifesto narrows markedly the sexual spectrum implied in the *Fortnightly* version of the argument, which seemed to advocate sexual expression within and outside of marriage and not to rule out Greek love:

> The loveliest object our art can represent . . . is the nude male or female figure. . . . Man is beautiful, woman is beautiful; both are most beautiful in the budding period and plenitude of their reproductive power. (Allen 1894, 388)

Like Symons, Sickert, Wedmore, Yeats and other male contributors to *The Yellow Book* and *The Savoy*, Allen celebrates the women of the theatre and music hall, but explicitly in relation to their bodies: 'We go to the theatre, in part to see and hear handsome men and winning women. The addition of ballet serves to accentuate this element in the enjoyment of theatrical entertainment. Take away sex, and the play were nothing' (Allen 1894, 389). And the hint of the homosocial is borne out in a subsequent juxtaposition between British Asceticism ('it teaches the money-grubbing and narrow-minded middle class . . . that love is a thing to be got over once for all in early life, and relegated to the back parlour of existence') and the example of Greece: 'Hellas knew better. The free Greek was not ashamed of sex, not ashamed of his own body, and its component members' (Allen 1894, 390).

Where the first parts of the *Fortnightly* article defined the 'new hedonism' in terms of its *freedom* – in reaction to the constraints of asceticism, the remainder attempts to delimit it:

> His object will always be so to use these functions as not to abuse them, either by enforced abstinence or by acquiescence in a hateful regime of vice, disease, and practical slavery for a large body of women. He knows that to be pure is not to be an anchorite, and that chastity means a profound disinclination to give the body where the heart is not given in unison (Allen 1894, 391)

However, as may be seen from this passage, the arguments are tantalisingly pluralist, with both abstinence and prostitution debarred, and purity allied with a chastity that is defined not legally, but simply as a union of sex and love. He offers a similarly fissured programme for responsible parenthood; tinctured with eugenics, it includes a mysterious declaration 'We will not doom to forced celibacy half our finest mothers' (Allen 1894, 392).

That my own mystification concerning Allen's position was shared may be seen in two articles which appeared in *The Humanitarian*, one by the Rev. Professor T.G. Bonney, attacking it from a Christian position and exposing its ambiguities (and ambivalences), and one by Allen himself in which he ridicules Bonney and pities 'poor Christianity' (Allen 1894a, 181) but also clarifies one strand of his argument by coming out as an ally of Josephine Butler and W.T. Stead 'I am a Social Purity man' (Allen 1894a, 184). In parallel, his advocacy of the body and of sexuality in line with the younger generation of sexologists such as Edward Carpenter, and Havelock Ellis who wrote for *The Savoy*, still stands. Homosexuality, the last aspect of the gender spectrum of the day aired in *The Humanitarian*'s portion of The New Hedonism debate, is found in George Ives' 'The New Hedonism Controversy.' This is one of the most open and sustained *public* defences of love between men in the press of the period, and it is noteworthy that *The Humanitarian* published it. Moreover, it is signed. Ives immediately aligns himself with 'those of the New Morality' (Ives 1894, 292), and takes advantage of the space Allen opens up by his use of the term hedonism, and his reference to Greek love. Basing his defence of 'the New Morality' on the authority of classical culture – 'It could have been no mean and unworthy ideal of love which was followed by so many of the master minds, by Solon and Demosthenes, by Alexander and Epaminondas, by Pindar and by Sophocles' (Ives 1894, p. 295) – he also claims a modern tradition which includes Whitman, George Grote, Pater and Symonds. How, Ives asks, can Hedonists logically denounce particular phases of sensuality? In April the case for the homosocial had been put pseudonymously in *The Artist* in 'The New Chivalry', by Kains Jackson the editor, who was forced to resign for carrying it.[5]

The New Hedonism debate, simultaneous with the first issues of *The Yellow Book*, maps the terrain of sexuality and gender in which both feature. Allen, initiator of the debate, never contributed to the quarterly, but his publisher – John Lane, and his illustrator – Beardsley, implicate him in the cultural formation to which it belonged. Lane's 'Hill-Top series' in which Allen's *The Woman Who Did* (1895) appeared was one which 'raises a protest in favour of purity,' and Allen's best selling if uneasy intervention in the genre of new woman fiction was contested by feminists such as Millicent Fawcett. The array of 90s texts and positions in the New Hedonism debate together with the new

[5] Letters of spring 1894 in the Clark Library from Arthur Douglas to Kains Jackson confirm the latter as author of 'The New Chivalry.' See for example Douglas to Kains Jackson, Autograph Letter, 16 May 1894. For more on *The Artist* see Fletcher, 1979, pp. 188–91, and Pittock 1993, 168.

woman fiction of the 90s by women and men indicate the cultural formations and the discourse of gender into which *The Yellow Book* and *The Savoy* move.

II. *Decadence and Journalism*

'And a weird word has been invented to explain the whole business. Decadence, decadence: you are all decadent nowadays.'
(*The Yellow Book* II, 1894, 266)

By the time Hubert Crackanthorpe wrote these words in the second issue of *The Yellow Book*, decadence had a history; denounced by Richard Le Gallienne earlier in the decade, the phenomenon was also attacked in house in the opening number's 'Reticence in Literature' written by Arthur Waugh. Crackanthorpe's 'Roundabout Remarks' were a reply to Waugh, part of a structure of contestation devised by the editors, by which Vol. II contained critiques of Vol. I. The *terms* in which this debate is conducted in *The Yellow Book* are as instructive as they are unexpected in a periodical whose name and design were calculated to buy into the cultural aura of *jaune* – provocative French fiction and down-market British railway novels. What Waugh calls for in *this* yellow book is **reticence** in fiction, an alliance between art and morality. What he denounces and what Crackanthorpe defends is realism in fiction, which Crackanthorpe terms the move back to Nature. It is this principle, and only secondarily the *styles* or artifice by which we tend to define decadence, which serves Crackanthorpe in selecting his examples: 'Ibsen, Degas, the New English Art Club; Zola, Oscar Wilde, and the Second Mrs. Tanqueray. Mr. Richard Le Gallienne is hoist with his own petard; even the British playwright has not escaped the taint' (Crackanthorpe 1894, 266). In the same number Max Beerbohm settles for Artifice as the sign of Decadence and celebrates it slyly:

There are signs that our English literature has reached that point, when, like the literatures of all the nations that have been, it must fall at length into the hands of the decadents. The qualities that I tried in my essay to travesty – paradox and marivaudage, lassitude, a love of horror and all unusual things, a love of argot and archaism and the mysteries of style – are not all these displayed, some by one, some by another of les jeunes ecrivains? Who knows but that Artifice is in truth at our gates and that soon she may pass through our streets?

Already the windows of Grub Street are crowded with watchful evil faces. They are ready, the men of Grub Street, to pelt her, as they have pelted all that came before her. Let them come down while there is still time, and hang their houses with colours, and strew the road with flowers. Will they not, for once, do homage to a new queen?

(Beerbohm 1894b, 284)

Evidence shows that the term 'decadence' is unstable. Arthur Symons, *Yellow Book* stalwart and *Savoy* editor, was one of its earliest explicators: in November 1893, six months before *The Yellow Book*, his 'The Decadent Movement in Literature' appeared in *Harper's*, but by 1898 when he published *The Symbolist Movement in Literature* he had subsumed it into symbolism, or deemed it overtaken. The constructions of decadence since – by Holbrook Jackson, G.K. Thornton, Ian Fletcher, Elaine Showalter, and John Stokes, to name but a few – share a common desire to clarify its meanings and a diversity of emphases. The defining mode of Symons' timely essay, the accessibility and the multi-valence of 'yellow', and the discourse and structures of the magazine itself (Waugh's 'Reticence' was followed in Vol. I by Crackanthorpe's 'Modern Melodrama')[6] indicate the extent to which *The Yellow Book* was a self-conscious player in the performance of Decadence.

The Yellow Book was a hard-covered quarterly periodical which ran for thirteen numbers between April 1894 and April 1897. It was initially edited by Henry Harland (letterpress) and Aubrey Beardsley (art) and, just as crucially, published by John Lane,[7] renown for the aesthetic design and fine production of his list, which featured prominently in the quarterly's adverts at the back. Its first five volumes published the work of a number of visual artists and writers associated with that hybrid formation called 'decadence', among them younger figures such as Ella d'Arcy, Aubrey Beardsley, Max Beerbohm, A.C. Benson, Hubert Crackanthorpe, John Davidson, George Egerton, Will Rothenstein, Evelyn Sharp, Arthur Symons, Netta Syrett, more established ones such as Henry Harland, Walter Sickert and P. Wilson Steer, and public figures such as Edmund Gosse, George Moore, and Frederick

6 'Modern Melodrama' is a sordid tale set in a bedroom at the moment of diagnosis of fatal consumption of a prostitute/actress; also present are her Cockney maid who has long expository speeches in dialect, and her current swell.
7 After the first two numbers which were published by the partners Elkin Mathews and John Lane, the partnership broke up, with Lane remaining in Vigo Street as The Bodley Head, the new imprint of *The Yellow Book*.

Leighton. Impressionism, feminism, naturalism, dandyism, symbolism, and classicism all participate in the politics of decadence in the 90s, and in *The Yellow Book*. In April 1895 Beardsley was dramatically extirpated from the periodical by Lane during the committal of Oscar Wilde, who was mistakenly associated with the periodical by the public: the yellow book Wilde was observed to be carrying was a French novel, and the contributors to *The Yellow Book* had never included Wilde.[8] In the event Beardsley's departure proved doubly harmful. By January 1896 Beardsley and Arthur Symons published *The Savoy*, a rival which was cheaper, better produced, and livelier than its competitor. Without Beardsley, and a number of his friends who transferred to *The Savoy*, the quality of *The Yellow Book* **was** different, safer if not worse, and it ceased publication without warning or explanation two years later, one number after the demise of its rival.

I want to suggest that the textual politics of *The Yellow Book* were eclectic from the outset, looking back to the reign of the quarterlies and invoking high Art and Literature, but at the same time participating in the discourses of the new journalism, the new woman, the new culture, and the new art. The orientation of the journal – recuperating the cultural values and production of the first half of the century, or adopting the present cultures of the 'new' – was contested in its pages, in both the letterpress and art. To resist the present (as do James and Arthur Waugh), or to embrace it – through appropriation (Beardsley), critique (d'Arcy), or celebration (Hubert Crackanthorpe) – these are reiterated positions which mark the first four numbers of *The Yellow Book*. The exclusion of Beardsley in April 1895 and the capitulation to the 'readers,'[9] represent the rise to dominance of certain conservative discourses of *The Yellow Book* there from the start: these involve the politics of literature, art, journalism, and gender. In important ways, the project of *The Yellow Book* looked back to pre-reform Britain and the great quarterly reviews, and forward to the success of the new (and illustrated) journalism with its millions of new readers. The resultant appeal of the magazine to different, targeted groups of consumer was in part the result of the publisher's projection of potential readership. That

[8] Wilde had been barred from the beginning on Beardsley's request.
[9] These readers were and are variously constructed, as 'the mob'; as middle-class, homophobic contributors in a moment of (national) male panic; as 'Mrs Grundy', the gendered typology of the respectable middle-class reader/ consumer and the butt of male writers' critique since 1885 in George Moore's 'Literature at Nurse.'

in April 1895, *The Yellow Book* attempted to resolve these tensions by excising the 'new' not only helps to explain its failure to survive, but illuminates the fragilities of nineties decadence, and the transgressiveness of the 'aesthetic' even at the end of the century. In the history of 'new journalism' in the 1890s the short life of *The Yellow Book*, poised as it was between the old and the new, may be set beside other radical serials (such as T.P. O'Connor's daily, *The Star*) which were also forced by the nature of the new market, the 'demos,' to abandon radical politics (Goodbody 1988). In the case of *The Yellow Book* the hysterical homophobia of 'readers' was shared by the periodical's contributors, some of whom were equally convinced and vociferous that the publication must be visibly purged of any association with Wildean Decadence.

III.   The Yellow Book *and* The New Woman

I want to consider *The Yellow Book* not as it is often viewed, as part of the avant-garde, 'non-commercial' art press, but in terms of the new journalism, the new woman, and the 'new culture', subjects which obsess its contributors, pervade its discourses, and determine its modes of production, its circulation, and its readership. First published in 1894, between the naming of the new journalism by Matthew Arnold in 1887 and the appearance of the *Daily News* in 1896, *The Yellow Book* both reacts against and appropriates aspects of the 'new journalism.' And appearing in the precise year that Ann Ardis (1990, 12) identifies with a shift in attention from the social phenomenon of the New Woman to its literary form in the New Women *novel*, *The Yellow Book* is timed to articulate the anxieties of its culture about the subjects of Woman and the Woman Writer. From its first piece in its first number in which a character notes nervously 'in the age we live in one gets lost among the genders' (James, 44) to the voicing of male panic in Vol. IV.

> Every bush and every bug grows its own specialist, and yet we, the patient and long-suffering-public, are left to endure both the fogs that make of London one murky pit, and the redundant female birth rate which threatens more revolution than all the forces of the Anarchists in active combination (A Woman 1894, 15)

The Yellow Book addresses the subject of Woman. These inscriptions are interactive within the magazine, and with writing outside it, part of a male and misogynist discourse of wit around the subject of the Woman Writer.

The first appears in Henry James' 'The Death of the Lion,' which refers to a literary culture in which the phenomenon of women writers with male pseudonyms is extended satirically to male novelists taking female names.[10] The second appears in a parallel keynote article in Vol. III, 'Woman – Wives *or* Mothers? By a Woman', attributed generically to a female author but written in fact by a man, Frederic Greenwood, an experienced and now a conservative journalist who had most recently founded *The Anti-Jacobin*, a journal like *The Oldie*, predicated on a reactionary position.[11] Thus, *The Yellow Book* realised James's ridiculous projection of a male author taking a female pseudonym and, still echoing James, alluded by this attribution to the spectacle of the anti-New Woman woman, an object of male gaze calculated to assuage male panic. At the same time, the article blatantly celebrates the sexualized woman – with the division of 'wives' and 'mothers' a domesticated reiteration of the Magdalene-Mary model; this position is such a familiar construct in the period that the article identifies its genre, satire, if not its gender through the extremity of its 'modest proposal[s]'. It also covertly displaces the female writer with the male, usurping the female authority it claims, and reproduces structures of male power through the imposition of a male gaze and discourse. By contrast, a female satire of '90s male fantasies about the woman writer may be seen in Sarah Grand's *The Heavenly Twins*; it appeared just before *The Yellow Book* which carried adverts for the publication of its 35th 1000; like James, Grand links the new woman with the popular press, but unlike him she validates the power of the female writer by figuring *her* as the victim of male physical abuse, rather than the female perpetrator of socio/cultural violence against the male artist:

> now, if you hit a woman, she'll put you in *Punch*, or revile you in the Dailies. Magazine you; write you down an ass in a novel; blackguard you in choice language from a public platform; or paint a picture of you which will make you wish you had never been born. Ridicule! They ridicule you. That's the worst of it. (Grand 1992, 273)

---

[10] In his story Henry James parodies in 'Guy Walsingham' one of Lane's most famous authors, George Egerton (Mary Dunne), who in the preceding year had published a best selling collection of short stories, *Keynotes*, on which Lane had built a series of books. James' 'Dora Forbes' (a male author) is his rococo reversal of the male pseudonym phenomenon.

[11] Toward the beginning of his career in 1865, Greenwood helped found the *Pall Mall Gazette,* which was modelled on a late eighteenth-century journal called *The Anti-Jacobin.*

There is no question, as Fraser Harrison notes, that Woman is one of the great subjects of *The Yellow Book*. From its immediate visual and commodified appeal as a coffee-table *book*, and the prominence of its drawings of the female subject – Beardsley's poster-art party goer on the cover and piano player on the title page complemented by draped neo-classical figures of Frederic Leighton's – these *Yellow Book* illustrations ushered in the female reader to Henry James's short story 'The Death of the Lion.' It, in turn, might be said to construct that reader as perpetrator-associate of the women readers in the tale who lionise, domesticate and then kill the caged, male, author-artist forcibly separated from the nurturing wild. That the harm lies in the female gaze itself is indicated by the fact that the only woman in the story who remains innocent of this Medusa role is Fanny Hurter who eradicates her desire to look at and reify the male artist, and accepts the passive role of *absence* and significantly, denial of proximity to the Author, and the substitution of the austerity of the impersonal 'oeuvre.' No male character in the story is similarly kept out of view of the male object. Male readers have more productive and/or active roles to choose from: nurturer-protector, journalist-attacker, and of course victim-creative artist. But the women and their domesticity are the reader-killers, and the narrator-protector who vies unsuccessfully with the female lion-tamers/menagerie keepers is male:

> I had a battle with Mrs. Wimbush over the artist she protected, and another over the question of a certain week, at the end of July, that Mr. Paraday appeared to have contracted to spend with her in the country. I protested against this visit; I intimated that he was too unwell for hospitality without a *nuance*, for caresses without imagination; I begged he might rather take the time in some restorative way. A sultry air of promises, of reminders hung over his August, and he would greatly profit by the interval of rest. He had not told me he was ill again – that he had had a warning; but I had not needed this, and I found his reticence his worst symptom. The only thing he said to me was that he believed a comfortable attack of something or other would set him up: it would put out of the question everything but the exemptions he prized. I am afraid I shall have presented him as a martyr in a very small cause if I fail to explain that he surrendered himself much more liberally than I surrendered him. He filled his lungs, for the most part, with the comedy of his queer fate: the tragedy was in the spectacles through which I chose to look.
>
> (James 1894, 38)

Aspects of this configuration of relations between the sexes recur in the first volume of *The Yellow Book*, in the two dramas for example, in Ella D'Arcy's short story 'Irremediable,' in Arthur Waugh's critical article 'Reticence in Literature,' and in the young Max Beerbohm's frolic 'A Defence of Cosmetics.' 'Irremediable' for example is a tale of a chance meeting and ill-judged marriage between a literate, reading, urban clerk and an illiterate country girl; it is married life which quickly becomes intolerable by virtue of their educational and intellectual inequality to which the title refers. In 'Reticence' Waugh winds up his assault on realism with an attack on the woman writer:

> But the latest development of literary frankness is, I think, the most insidious and fraught with the greatest danger to art. A new school has arisen which combines the characteristics of effeminacy and brutality. In its effeminate aspect it plays with the subtler emotions of sensual pleasure, on its brutal side it has developed into that class of fiction which for want of a better word I must call chirurgical. . . . In fiction it infects its heroines with acquired diseases of names unmentionable, and has debased the beauty of maternity by analysis of the process of gestation. Surely the inartistic temperament can scarcely abuse literature further. I own I can conceive nothing less beautiful. . . .
> We are told that this is a part of the revolt of woman, and certainly our women-writers are chiefly to blame. It is out of date, no doubt, to clamour for modesty; but the woman who describes the sensations of childbirth does so, it is to be presumed – not as the writer of advice to a wife – but as an artist producing literature for art's sake. And so one may fairly ask her: How is art served by all this? What has she told us that we did not all know, or could not learn from medical manuals? and what impression has she left us over and above the memory of her unpalatable details? (Waugh 1894b, 218–9)

If the first number of the new quarterly begins with James' onslaught on women readers, it ends with the first act of a play 'The Fool's Hour,' co-authored by John Oliver Hobbes [Mrs Craigie] and George Moore, an attack on the dulness and constraints of marriage (that of the Doldrummonds), and a paean to the delights of bachelor life as lived by their son. In the opening scene Lord D. greets his old friend 'the existence which my wife enjoys, and which I have learnt to endure, would not suit every one' (Hobbes and Moore 1894, 254) and then exhorts him

> Ah, thank heaven every night and morning , my dear Digby, that you are a bachelor. Praying for sinners and breeding them would seem

the whole duty of man. I was no sooner born than my parents were filled with uneasiness lest I should not live to marry and beget an heir of my own. Now I have an heir, his mother will never know peace until she has found him a wife!

(Hobbes and Moore 1894, 255)

As their son Cyril leaves for the theatre, in anticipation of his plan to set up chambers in town, he echoes his father in his explanation: 'I cannot see much of the world through my mother's embroidery.' This is the last scene of the act.

These by no means exhaust the forms misogyny takes in *The Yellow Book*, nor is misogyny the only gender marker of the magazine. Homosocial and erotic discourse are inscribed in A.C. Benson's poem which is dedicated to another contributor E[dmund] G[osse], as well as in James' first story and in Beerbohm's 'Defence of Cosmetics', in which 'Max' takes the opportunity to note those 'countless gentlemen who walk about town . . . artificially bronzed' and men 'who make themselves up, seemingly with an aesthetic purpose' (Beerbohm 1894a, 78). The naturalism which characterises stories in *The Yellow Book* by Ella D'Arcy and Hubert Crackanthorpe and informs Arthur Symons' poem 'Stella Maris' also foregrounds male as well as female (hetero)sexuality, and reiterates a pattern of sexual relations between upper class men and working class, 'fallen,' or theatrical women. Beardsley's drawings of actresses and prostitutes (e.g. 'Mrs Patrick Campbell' and 'Night Piece' in Vol. I) often display women and their bodies as objects of the gaze of the (implied) male spectator, in profile for example, or in telling contrast to each other ('L'Education Sentimentale'), or as objects of leering male (and sometimes female) creatures. The representation of sexuality and a full spectrum of gender is pervasive in Beardsley's visual and verbal work.

By contrast with Beardsley's (and Beerbohm's) appropriation of theatricality for decadence, Sickert's 'The Old Oxford Music Hall' takes a gendered subject – the music hall (see especially Arthur Symons and Frederick Wedmore in the *Savoy*, and Lautrec's poster art) – and treats it as a vast architectural study, with its depiction of the music hall artiste so distanced as to be dwarfed and only broadly suggested, if central. Certainly, Sickert's is one of a number of non-participant pictures in the discourse of gender in *The Yellow Book*, but that discourse nevertheless remains the most reiterated in pictures and letterpress in the early volumes of *The Yellow Book*.

I want to indicate briefly how the subject of women was constructed in the period in which *The Yellow Book* first appeared. In January 1894 the *Nineteenth Century* which habitually fostered debate through its symposium structures initiated a series of articles 'The Revolt of the Daughters' which ran monthly to March; the first contributor was Blanche Crackanthorpe,[12] who offered qualified support for the young New Women; she was followed in February by a dialogue, 'Mothers and Daughters,' which developed her case; signed *Mrs* Frederic Harrison, the format echoes Mr Frederic Harrison's renowned 'Culture: a Dialogue.' In March, the mothers (Crackanthorpe and Haweis) were at it again, and only then were two daughters (Alys Pearsall Smith and Kathleen Cuffe) permitted to publish their own defence. Also in March, two fresh series of articles began, stimulated by pieces which raised related issues: Sarah Grand's 'The New Aspects of the Woman Question' which appeared in *The North American Review*, and Grant Allen's 'The New Hedonism.' As detailed above, the 'New Hedonism' debate shifted to the *Humanitarian* and ran from August to October, while Ouida, replying to Sarah Grand in the May *NAR* seems to have capitalised the phrase New Woman for the first time (Ardis 1990, 11). And November's *Fortnightly*, perhaps to win over its progressive women readers who had objected to Allen's 'New Hedonism,' carried 'Women's Newspapers' by Evelyn March Phillipps cited above.

Preceding this flurry of 1894 debate were three volumes of fiction dealing with the Woman Question in 1893, George Egerton's [Mary Dunne's] short stories, *Keynotes*, published by John Lane and trailed by the renown Keynote series, Sarah Grand's multi-edition best seller *The Heavenly Twins* (Grant Richards (3 vol. edn and then Heinemann), and George Gissing's *The Odd Women*. In 1895 during the run of *The Yellow Book*, Lane's list included two novels by Allen, *The British Barbarians* and the bestseller *The Woman Who Did*. When Thomas Hardy's *Jude the Obscure* appeared serially in 1894–5, with its new woman figure of Sue Brideshead and its discussion of divorce, responses were so vituperative that Hardy vowed to desist from writing fiction again. In every field of contemporary writing, in newspapers and magazines, in short fiction and the novel, in John Lane's list, and thus unsurprisingly in *The Yellow Book* itself, the Woman Question and the New Woman, and questions of gender more generally were among the impinging subjectivites of the day.

---

[12] Hubert Crackanthorpe, author of naturalist fiction in *The Yellow Book* and other '90s magazines, was Blanche Crackanthorpe's son.

IV.   *The New Journalism*

I want now to turn to a second formative discourse and cultural formation of the period in which *The Yellow Book* participated, and that is the new journalism. As it happens, there is a journal closely linked with *The Yellow Book* which, prior to the declaration of a new series, undertook public self-scrutiny and an economically induced remodelling in January and February 1894, just in the period of the run up to the first volume of *The Yellow Book*. It was the monthly *New Review* (1889–97), a periodical which shares a number of contributors – including James, Crackanthorpe, Gosse, Benson, Saintsbury, Le Gallienne, R. Garnett, and Symons with *The Yellow Book*. But the most obvious link between the two publications is *Yellow Book* regular Arthur Waugh, writer of 'Reticence in Literature' in Vol. I, who functioned as Deputy Editor of *The New Review* in 1894, helping Archibald Grove through his final year as editor. Their announcements to their readers in the January and February numbers provide an excellent view of the periodical market and the new journalism at a time when both publications were attempting to consolidate their positions. There are a number of salient points of comparison. It should be said that from the first in 1889 the *New Review* saw itself as tapping a new readership associated with the new journalism, and this was reflected in its attempt to rival the *Nineteenth Century* and the *Fortnightly* by matching their weightiness at a fraction of their price. By 1894 it was setting its sights at *The Review of Reviews*, W.T. Stead's 90s project, and proposing to introduce quality illustrations. In its remarks about its new design, its address to the staple projection of the new journalism audience, the railway traveller, and to the visually discerning reader are notable, and anticipate *The Yellow Book's* similar attention to design and quality: 'The general get-up will be improved both as regards the paper and the cover, and in order to facilitate the reading of the magazine for those who are travelling, the edges will be cut' (Anon. 1894e, [128]). In the quotations that follow, reference to the archaic status of quarterlies, the potential educated audience, and the strategy of quality illustrations as distinct from popular fodder all have resonance in relation to *The Yellow Book*:

The New Review will be the first review which will be regularly illustrated – in no way competing with any existing magazines, not being merely a series of interviews sandwiched between fiction, but a serious review, in which the illustrations will form an actual integral part, really illustrative accompaniment to the articles included. For that reason, naturally, the part devoted to fiction cannot be illustrated. . . . *The New Review* in no way becomes an illustrated magazine, but remains what it has been hitherto, – a Review devoted to the great problems of the day. (Anon. 1894d)

It is true that with the easy methods of transmission through the post office, railroads, etc., the old quarterlies have been in a great way replaced by monthly reviews. But they have been for the most part, too expensive, frequently too 'special,' and only occasionally sufficiently attractive to appeal to the enormous reading public that has grown up out of a liberal legislation in educational matters. That the mere 'interview' and personal gossip sandwiched between ephemeral fiction, and illustrated by cheap process, would not permanently and entirely satisfy this growing and intelligent audience, soon became manifest, and the avidity with which the *Review of Reviews* was taken up at the outset, proved that there were hundreds and thousands who were eager to inform themselves on all the topics discussed in those severer organs. (Anon. 1894e, [127])

The last point of comparison is also telling, the plan of the *Review* to introduce every month 'one very carefully selected short story,' in addition to the illustrations, thus 'dintinguish[ing] it from any existing periodical' (Anon. 1894d). With its introduction of the short story, of quality illustration, of improved production, and its address to a newly educated audience, *The New Review's* project represents the market at the moment of *The Yellow Book's* intervention.

'The Death of the Lion,' Henry James' *Yellow Book* story in April 1894 could be said to parallel Gissing's *New Grub Street* (1891) in its pitting of art and literature against the new journalism; its satiric element attaches grimly to the editors, reporters, and their organs – Mr Deedy, Mr Pinhorn, Mr Morrow, and the *Empire*, and much of the imagery of debasement and de-valuation stems from the rhetoric of the press:

The big blundering newspaper had discovered him, and now he was proclaimed and anointed and crowned. . . . The article was a date; he had taken rank at a bound. . . . When Neil Paraday should come out of the house he would come out a contemporary. That was what had happened – the poor man was to be squeezed into his horrible age. (James 1894, 17)

Contempt for the new journalism and its contrast to literature are formally inscribed by transferring the vocabulary attaching to the journalistic commodity to the author himself:

> His book sold but moderately, though the article in *The Empire* had done unwonted wonders for it; but he circulated in person in a manner that the libraries might well have envied (James 1894, 25)

This figure of circulation functions as a motif in the novella, moving from the writer himself, to a hilarious account of his two volume novel at a house party (41) to the dissonant account of the fatal loss of a unique manuscript which 'circulates' from the author to his hostess to a guest to a maid to a valet to Lord Doriment who leaves it on a train. Circulation of his book at the house is as follows:

> There is supposed to be a copy of his last book in the house, and in the hall I come upon ladies, in attitudes, bending gracefully over the first volume. I discreetly avert my eyes, and when I next look round the precarious joy has been superseded by the book of life. There is a sociable circle or a confidential coup, and the relinquished volume lies open on its face, as if it had been dropped under extreme coercion. Somebody else present finds it and transfers it, with its air of momentary desolation, to another piece of furniture. Every one is asking every one about it all day, and every one is telling every one where they put it last. I'm sure it's rather smudgy about the twentieth page. I have a strong impression too that the second volume is lost – has been packed in the bag of some departing guest; and yet everybody has the impression that somebody else has read to the end. You see therefore that the beautiful book plays a great part in our conversation. (James 1894, 41).

On the circulation of the manuscript, the narrator comments 'One would think it was some thrilling number of *The Family Budget*' (47). But despite the elements of the ridiculous and the comic, the accounts of circulation build ominously until the loss of the manuscript is parallelled by nothing less than the death of the famous author. James' short story itself has characteristics of the new journalism, its fragmentation into bite-size parts for example, to increase accessibility. But immediately upon opening *The Yellow Book*, James' story alerts us to consciousness of the proximity of the new journalism and its construction as an irresistible enemy.

Many other elements of *The Yellow Book* relate to the new journalism. Perhaps, the most obvious relation is a negative one, in the publisher's and editors' choice of the archaic format of the quarterly, at the very moment in the history of journalism when topicality and up-to-dateness seemed paramount. Designed to remove the periodical from the affray for the 'busy reader' of W.T. Stead's publications such as *The Review of Reviews*, the quarterly *Yellow Book* was apparently endorsing the values of James' narrator in denying the topical, the personal, the interview, and the mass appeal of the vulgar and commodified writing in which terms the new journalism was constructed. Arthur Waugh, soon a prominent contributor to Vol. I, writing for *The Critic* announced the new project in its earliest stage as follows:

> It has yet to be proved that the public will buy literature for its own sake: the timely and journalistic contents of our monthly reviews show how keenly editors appreciate the necessity for the interest of the passing hour. And the present moment . . . is the one thing which will *not* be consulted in *The Yellow Book*.
>
> (Quoted in Mix, 71; Waugh 1894a, 43)

And when it appeared in April, its format attracted attention: 'The first volume of the *Yellow Book* (Mathews and Lane), an illustrated quarterly, evidently aims at novelty' but significantly the *Athenaeum* singles out its illustrations and links it to gift annuals, a highly commodified if long established form: 'and yet it is not unlike in appearance the annual volumes of *Chatterbox* and other periodicals for young people' (Anon. 1894a, 509). *The Saturday Review* makes a similar point, but introduces an additional association – with women, which makes the link with the attempt by the new journalism to widen readership and in particular to provide for women readers. The element of 'pictures' independent of letterpress, and thus *not* illustration, has perhaps drawn our attention to the alliance of *The Yellow Book* with the Fine Art press, and away from the popular illustrated magazine, but as contemporary criticism shows, the latter association was uppermost at the time:

> The new illustrated quarterly, *The Yellow Book* (Mathews & Lane), if not precisely the book of beauty and the beautiful book we had been led to anticipate, comprises certain good matters that will engage the discriminating taste. . . . The illustrations of *The Yellow Book* are, like woman's love, a thing apart, and certainly do not justify its existence, while the get up of the book is curiously unlovely, and like the children's Christmas picture books in appearance.
>
> (Anon. 1894b, 455)

From the robustly male-reader position of *The Saturday Review* critic the 'get-up of the book' feminises and even infantilises the project, increasing its accessibility beyond male generic comfort to those whom Sarah Grand identifies among periodical readers as 'the shy little girls in the old-fashioned houses, who never looked at anything in the magazines but the pictures and the poetry' (Grand 1992, 366). While therefore the subject of women in *The Yellow Book* is fraught with anxiety and misogyny, female readers seem to be among the audience addressed by its 'get-up' and illustrated format, if not the contents of many of the illustrations. At the same time the critic signals to male connoisseurs that Vol.I does cater for them to some extent, that it 'comprises certain good matters' for the 'discriminating taste.' It is perhaps the disappointment of expectations of male connoisseurs of both Art and the erotic that is inscribed in these critiques of the first number of *The Yellow Book*.

The address of many of these illustrations, Beardsley's especially, *and* of much of the letterpress is also a function of perhaps the most castigated aspect of the new journalism, sensationalism. March Phillipps dramatises its importance in a contemporary article on the new journalism in *The New Review*: 'An editor of considerable standing said lately to a contributor, "I don't want wit, I don't want fancy, I don't even want grammar. Give me sensation" ' (March Phillipps 1894b, 188). Although the name of *The Yellow Book*, its subjectivities, and its illustrations have most often been associated with what numerous contributors to *The Yellow Book*, from Arthur Waugh (1894b, 216) to Hubert Crackanthorpe have called Decadent, these same elements of the production of *The Yellow Book* are in keeping with the rhetoric of sensation, designed to create large readerships seeking titillation through writing which is commodified as 'news' through its notoriety. Despite its attempt to give itself weight and distance through its quarterly (in)frequency, and despite its claim to publish Literature and Art rather than journalism, much of *The Yellow Book* avails itself of the rhetoric of sensationalism, including its name, its poster-art cover, and its decision to publish in *one* volume such provocative pieces as Arthur Symons' 'Stella Maris', Beerbohm's spoof on cosmetics, Waugh's diatribe on reticence, and Beardsley's drawings 'L'Education Sentimentale' and 'Night Piece'. Even its name may have carried greater notoriety to male connoisseurs than a generic reference to French yellow back and railway fiction may suggest; for those who had read Wilde's *Picture of Dorian Gray*, the specific allusion would be to the passage on the 'poisonous book' which begins 'His eye fell on the yellow book that Lord Henry had sent him' (Wilde 1981, 125). Part of the sensationalism of *The Yellow Book* functions in the marketplace as a new journalism technique of enhancing sales among the bourgeois reader whom it is designed to titillate and attract.

The price of *The Yellow Book* too looks to the old and the new readers and markets. By this time in the century, when monthly reviews were selling for about 2 shillings to 2s 6d, magazines for 1 shilling, and old (expensive) quarterlies for 6 shillings, the 5 shillings of *The Yellow Book* is toward the upper end of the market for periodicals. However, as a cloth bound *book*, it was priced at a shilling less than cloth bound, one-volume novels at 6 shillings. Neither the old quarterlies nor the one-volume novels, were likely to be copiously illustrated, and if they were, neither the quality and quantity of their illustrations were likely to match those of *The Yellow Book*. Poised between the periodical press and the book as *The Yellow Book* was, it may not have appeared costly to its targeted readership, although it should be noted that after *The Savoy* appeared in January 1896, in *paper* covers but quarterly at 2s 6d, *The Yellow Book*'s attachment to the *book* format may have begun to appear inflexible and retrograde, which in some respects it was.

I have argued that a conservative strain of *Yellow Book* politics and contributors is there from the outset, and Henry James' and Arthur Waugh's pejorative juxtaposition of literature and journalism, books and periodicals is echoed; while writing in the latter they prefer the former. Even the undergraduate Max Beerbohm denigrated journalism in his tongue-in-cheek riposte to critics of his 'Defence of Cosmetics': 'how far is it [criticism] reformatory. Personally, I cannot conceive how any artist can be hurt by remarks dropped from a garret into a gutter' (Beerbohm 1894b, 282). However, Beardsley dissents. From his art it is clear that Beardsley's cultural politics looked far more appreciatively to the commodity culture associated with the new journalism. In July 1894's *New Review* he contributes a celebration of adverts to a forum on that 1890s art form, 'The Art of the Hoarding': 'London will soon be resplendent with advertisements, and against a leaden sky skysigns will trace their formal arabesque. Beauty has laid siege to the city, and telegraph wires shall no longer be the sole joy of our aesthetic perceptions' (Beardsley 1894, 54). It is significant of *The Yellow Book*'s view of itself as a commodity participating in the market that it carried adverts, unlike *The Savoy*. Volume I ended with a substantial section of publishers' adverts, made up of 'The Yellow Book Advertisements' which comprised 18 pages of copy from seventeen publishers other than Mathews and Lane, and a second section of 17 pages devoted exclusively to the Mathews & Lane list, flanked by quotations from the press attesting to the beauty of their books. After the first volume however, the number of other publishers buying space diminished greatly, with six in Vol. II and five in Vol. III. That this continued fall in advertising was an index to its decreasing respectability is borne out by a critic referring to the contrast between the censored Vol. 5 denuded of its Beardsleys, and what preceded it:

Volume V of the mustard-coated quarterly, which comes to us with the lilac and laburnum, is amazingly proper. The 'Philerote' who gets his reading like his milk, in carts, may order it from Mudie's with confidence. The omniscient young person of this age of decadence need not blush to see it in the hands of her mother. Nay, more, it is so proper that it might, without seeming impropriety, be taken up the river in a boat and read, yellow and unashamed, beneath some overhanging willow, or on some riverside lawn (Anon. 1895)

Beerbohm's 'Letter to the Editor' in Vol. II was one of the ways the editors of *The Yellow Book* created serial formats which stressed continuities in a periodical which looked like a one-off book and appeared infrequently. Two other pieces in Vol. II 'reviewed' Vol. I, Hubert Crackanthorpe's rewriting of the issue of 'reticence' in literature as a reply to Waugh in Vol. I, and Philip G. Hamerton's formal critique of the 'Literature' and the 'Illustrations.' One of the genres for which *The Yellow Book* became renown was the short story, and this is partly a function of its quarterly (in)frequency which disallowed serial fiction, which the monthlies exploited as a strategy of serialisation. So, *The Yellow Book* had to create suspense and interest in its potential readership through means other than serial fiction. Beardsley's art, and works by other recurring authors and artists who constituted a core 'circle' helped create the serial identity of the journal, luring readers and purchasers to return to *The Yellow Book* after a three month interval.

Women readers, journalists and contributors were all addressed, constructed, and wooed by the new journalism, and it is unsurprising that *The Yellow Book* developed the writing career of Ella D'Arcy and published Charlotte Mew, George Egerton, John Oliver Hobbes, Olive Custance, Victoria Cross, E. Nesbit, Evelyn Sharp, Leila Macdonald, and Netta Syrett. Although the founders of *The Yellow Book* were all male, Ella D'Arcy did come as an initially unknown contributor to occupy a seat at the editorial centre. It is of some interest that in the various accounts of D'Arcy's career, however summary and brief, her personal (love) life invariably figures, as though implicitly to explain

her editorial position at *The Yellow Book*. There is no doubt however
that Ella D'Arcy did function for a period as Deputy Editor of *The Yellow
Book*; Alan Anderson's selection of her letters to Lane shows the
considerable power she had on occasion. It is arguable that Ella D'Arcy's
role as a journalist and editor on *The Yellow Book* relates to the culture
of journalism, the New Woman, and the New Journalism rather than
to any simply individual history of personal life. March Phillipps' piece
on 'Women's Newspapers' provides a timely overview of what by the
1890s is a history of women in journalism for 50 years, and the
unmistakeable address of W.T. Stead to women readers and potential
journalists in *The Review of Reviews* in the 1890s is the context of
D'Arcy's position. In November 1894 Woodhull's *Humanitarian* carried
a piece on 'Another Woman Editor':

> The fact that Mrs Frederick Arthur Beer has assumed the editorship
> of the *Sunday Times*, a journal of which she is the proprietor, adds
> one more to the list of women's successes in journalism. This is one
> of the most striking instances on this side of the Atlantic [ie Britain?],
> the *Sunday Times* being the only general newspaper that has a woman
> at its head. Mrs. Crawford, the Paris correspondent of the *Daily News*,
> is a name well-known in journalism, and quite recently 'Tasma,'
> Madame Couvreur, has been appointed Belgian correspondent to the
> *Times*, a post rendered vacant by the death of her husband. So far as
> we can judge of recent issues, the *Sunday Times* is already improving
> in tone and news, and has added many fresh features of interest.
>
> (Anon. 1894c, 401)

V. *The New Woman and the New Journalism*

How do the New Journalism and the New Woman as subjects conjoin
in *The Yellow Book*? James gives the lead in 'The Death of the Lion'
where Literature is explicitly linked to and *dependent* on a world free of
women, and the act of literary creation is sexualized and takes place
between men: it is 'an amorous plan' (James 1894, 13) to be carried out
in the protective 'encircling medium, tepid enough' (James 1894, 14)
of the artist's male companion, a convert from the new journalism. The
female keepers of the menagerie on the other hand, the women who
tame and kill the lion, are repeatedly, even insistently linked to the new
journalism; their leader, Mrs Weeks Wimbush 'was a blind violent force,
to which I could attach no more idea of responsibility than to the hum
of a spinning-top. It was difficult to say what she conduced to but to

circulation' (James 1894, 26). She is portrayed as an irresponsible organiser of puffing in the press, with her voracious manipulation of Art and Literature for social purposes linked to the commodification of Art and Literature by the press:

> She played her victims against each other with admirable ingenuity, and her establishment was a huge machine in which the tiniest and the biggest wheels went round to the same treadle. I had a scene with her in which I tried to express that the function of such a man was to exercise his genius – not to serve as a hoarding for pictorial posters. The people I was perhaps angriest with were the editors of magazines who had introduced what they called new features, so aware were they that the newest feature of all would be to make him grind their axes by contributing his views on vital topics and taking part in the periodical prattle about the future of fiction (James 1894, 37–8)

The positions of women in *The Yellow Book*, as contributors, editors, and subjects are likewise a function of the complex interaction of topical issues of gender, decadence, and the New Journalism in the mid 1890s.

Works Cited

d'Arcy, Ella, 1990. *Some Letters to John Lane*, ed. Alan Anderson, Edinburgh: The Tregara Press.

Allen, Grant, 1889. 'Plain Words on the Woman Question,' *Fortnightly Review* 46, Oct., 448–58.

———, 1894. 'The New Hedonism,' *Fortnightly Review* 55, March, 377–92.

———, 1894a. 'About the New Hedonism,' *Humanitarian* 5, September, 181–5.

Anon., 1894a. 'Our Library Table,' *Athenaeum* 3469, April 21, 509.

Anon., 1894b. 'New Books and Reprints,' *The Saturday Review* 77, April 28, 455.

Anon., 1894c. 'Another Woman Editor,' in 'Notes and Comments,' *The Humanitarian* 5, Nov., 401.

Anon. 1894d. 'Announcement,' *The New Review* 10, January, unnumbered page.

Anon. 1894e. 'Special Announcement,' *The New Review* 10, February, [127]

Anon. 1895. 'A Reformed Yellow Book,' newspaper cutting in Princeton University Library, source unknown.

Ardis, Ann, 1990. *New Women, New Novels*, New Brunswick, N.J., and London: Rutgers U.P.

A Woman [Frederic Grunwood], 1894. 'Women – Wives or Mothers?,' *The Yellow Book* III, Oct., 11–18.

Beardsley, Aubrey, 1894. 'The Art of the Hoarding. Part III,' *The New Review* 11, July, 53–4.

Beerbohm, Max, 1894a, 'A Defence of Cosmetics,' *The Yellow Book* I, April, 65–82.

——, 1894b. 'A Letter to the Editor,' *The Yellow Book* II, July, 281–4.

Bonney, T.G., 1894. 'The New Hedonism,' *Humanitarian* 5, August, 106–13.

Brake, Laurel, 1994. *Subjugated Knowledges*, London: Macmillan.

Crackanthorpe, Hubert, 1894. 'Reticence in Literature. Some Roundabout Remarks,' *The Yellow Book* II, July, 259–69.

Dellamora, Richard, 1990. *Masculine Desire*, Boston: Harvard U.P.

Dowling, Linda, 1979. 'The "Decadent" and the New Woman in the 1890s,' *Nineteenth Century Fiction*, March, 434–53.

Fletcher, Ian, 1979. 'Decadence and the Little Magazines,' *Decadence and the 1890s*, SUAS 17, London: Arnold, 172–202.

Goodbody, John, 1988. 'The *Star*: its Role in the Rise of the New Journalism' in *Papers for the Millions*, ed. Joel Wiener, Westport, CT: Greenwood, 143–63.

Grand, Sarah, 1992 (1893). *The Heavenly Twins*, Ann Arbor: University of Michigan Press.

Harrison, Fraser, ed., 1974. *The Yellow Book: An Anthology*, London, New York: St Martin's Press.

Ives, George, 1894. 'The New Hedonism Controversy,' *Humanitarian* 5, October, 292–7.

'P.C,' [Kains Jackson, Charles], 1894. 'The New Chivalry,' *The Artist and Journal of Home Culture*, April, 102–4.

March Phillipps, Evelyn, 1894a. 'Women's Newspapers,' *Fortnightly Review* 56, November, 661–70.

——, 1894b. 'The New Journalism,' *The New Review* 13, August, 82–9.

Mix, Katherine, 1960. *A Study in Yellow: The Yellow Book and its Contributors*, Lawrence: University of Kansas Press.

Pittock, Murray, 1993. *Spectrum of Decadence. The Literature of the 1890s*, London: Routledge.

Poovey, Mary, 1988. *Uneven Developments*, Chicago: University of Chicago Press.

Showalter, Elaine, 1991. *Sexual Anarchy*, London: Bloomsbury.

Stokes, John, 1989. *In the Nineties*, Hemel Hempstead: Harvester.

——, 1990. 'Dieppe: 1895,' *Essays and Poems in Memory of Ian Fletcher*, ELT Special Series No. 4, Greensboro, N.C., 11–23.

Tuchman, G., 1989. *Edging Women Out*, London: Routledge.

Walkowitz, Judith, 1992. *City of Dreadful Delight*, London: Virago.

Waugh, Arthur, 1894a. 'London Letter,' *The Critic* 21, 20 Jan., 42–3.

——, 1894b. 'Reticence in Literature,' *The Yellow Book* I, April, 201–19.

Wilde, Oscar, 1981 (1891). *The Picture of Dorian Gray*, ed. Isobel Murray, Oxford: OUP.

'Sterile Ecstasies':
The Perversity of the Decadent Movement

JOSEPH BRISTOW

I

'The latest movement in European literature', wrote Arthur Symons in 1893, 'has all the qualities that mark the end of great periods, the qualities that we find in the Greek, the Latin, decadence' (Symons 1893, 858). But no sooner had Symons made this influential claim in 'The Decadent Movement in Literature' than an unwelcome fate would befall the epithet on which he built his argument. For, in devising a suitable idiom to characterize the decisive shifts he detected in Belgian, English and French literature, Symons discovered that Decadence created more problems than it could categorically resolve. Not before long was Decadence condemned in nearly every quarter of the literary establishment. Even in *The Yellow Book*, the periodical closely associated with this movement, Hubert Crackenthorpe deplored how a 'weird word had been invented to explain' the 'miserable, inadequate age of ours'. 'Decadence, decadence', chanted Crackenthorpe in 1894, 'you are all decadent nowadays' (Crackenthorpe 1894, 266). Soon after in 1896, when Symons launched his rival journal, the *Savoy*, the editorial made this unequivocal announcement: 'We have no formula and we desire no false unity of form and matter . . . We are not Realists or Romanticists or Decadents' (Symons 1896, 127). Later, when the decade had almost run its course, Symons furnished a substantial Introduction to the book that would revise and expand many of the ideas about Impressionism and Symbolism he had outlined in his landmark essay of 1893. There he notes that 'something which is vaguely called Decadence had come into being', and he insists that the 'name, rarely used with any precise meaning, was usually hurled as a reproach or hurled back as a defence'. By this point, it was clear that the word had been altogether misappropriated, not least because it implied immorality of an unmentionable kind: 'It pleased some young men in various countries to call themselves Decadents, with all the thrill of unsatisfied virtue masquerading as uncomprehended vice'. Clearly averse to the depravity now contaminating the term, Symons adds that Decadence 'is in its place only when applied to style; to that ingenious deformation of the language . . . which can be compared with what we are accustomed to call the Greek and Latin of the Decadence' (Symons 1924, 102). Only by invoking classical precedents could Symons make a credible defence of the maligned name he had largely been responsible for passing into English culture.

But this was not a specious justification. In her comprehensive analysis of the Decadent interest in linguistic artificiality and autonomy, Linda C. Dowling shows how the short life of literary Decadence found its immediate antecedent in two influential works by Walter Pater – the novel, *Marius the Epicurean* (1885), and the revered essay on 'Style' (1889), both of which elaborate a theory of authorial self-consciousness. So it is not perhaps surprising to find Symons mentioning Pater's 'morbid curiosity of form' in 'The Decadent Movement in Literature' (Symons 1893, 867). Phrasing of this kind prompts Dowling to argue that the endeavour of literary Decadence lay in a serious intellectual project, one that shall only remain obscured if we continue to focus on the so-called 'yellow' or 'naughty' 1890s as a 'cultural episode with sensational or lurid overtones' (Dowling 1986, ix). She suggests that in Pater's novel it is the fascination with Euphuism in Apuleius' *Golden Ass* that feeds most directly into late-Victorian Decadent interest in the 'deformation' of the written word where the materiality of the sign departs entirely from Romantic assumptions about the living, if not divine, essence of the Logos. Euphuism, according to Pater in 'Style', arises when 'the literary conscience has been awakened to forgotten duties towards language, towards the instrument of expression' (Pater 1921, I 97). Not only manifest in Apuleius' work, but also in the Elizabethan writing of John Lyly and the poetry of the nineteenth-century 'French Romanticists' (such as Charles Baudelaire), Euphuism from Pater's perspective emerges when writers concentrate on the differing cultural heritages inhabiting the written word. Heterodox, freed from convention, able to combine archaism with 'neology', Euphuism heightens an author's linguistic self-consciousness by encouraging a creative attitude towards the mixed ancestry of English: 'Racy Saxon monosyllables, close to us as touch and sight, he will intermix readily with those long, savoursome, Latin words, rich in "second intention" ' (Pater 1913, 16). Dowling claims that the Paterian commitment to a burnished style was born out of deep-rooted crises in comparative philology, and that Euphuism presented a critical model for comprehending the possibility of linguistic renewal in the literature of his own era. (This interest, of course, is clearly displayed in Pater's

own memorable stylistic techniques.) But Pater, as father of the Aesthetes, would bequeath to the Decadent generation a precarious inheri-
tance. If Decadence brought about a distinctive apprehension of how
old and new vocabularies could be intermixed to reconfigure literary
practice, it could not in Symons' hands have taken recourse to a more
unfortuitous repertoire of terms. In 'The Decadent Movement in Literature' he keeps returning to one word that would certainly support
the popular view that the 1890s comprised nothing less than a period
exuding 'sensational or lurid overtones'. Time and again, Symons
alludes to the 'spiritual and moral perversity' of the 'supreme art' that
belonged to the Decadent movement (Symons 1893, 859). It is 'perversity' that, more than any other word in Symons' vocabulary, oscil-
lates uneasily between the aesthetic and erotic pre- occupations of
late-Victorian literary Decadence.

In examining the earliest formulations of the short-lived Decadent
era, the present discussion considers how Symons sought to legitimize
a form of perversity that was sexual as well as stylistic. Although it is a
critical commonplace to state that the hostility that greeted the trials
of Oscar Wilde meant that it would prove increasingly hard for Decadent writing to appear anything but immoral, this well-rehearsed
account can detract from Symons' fascination with the perverse nature
of male sexual desire, regardless of object choice. The violent reaction
against the erotic poetry he produced at the time shows how impossible
it was for Symons to elevate the compulsive longings of male heterosexuality as acceptable poetic subject-matter among his educated peers.
Even if Symons himself was not imprisoned for recording his sexual
encounters with female dancers in countless poems, he felt the full blast
of a disapproving readership in many influential periodicals. It is,
however, a mistake to think that he felt isolated in what he wanted to
achieve. For, as several of his essays reveal, he was highly responsive to
those whom he believed shared his interest in the pathological erotic
sensations of the male body. The trouble is that modern criticism has
had considerable difficulty in trying to comprehend why Symons
grouped such a motley crew of writers together under the same banner.
By returning to Symons' perversity, we can come to understand how
and why he believed that specific sexual and stylistic symptoms assuredly placed literary Decadence at the end of an epoch.

II

Surveying the evanescent life of literary Decadence, R.K.R. Thornton identifies two related events in 1895 signalling its downfall (Thornton 1983, 37–40). The first is the notorious appearance of Max Nordau's *Degeneration* in an English translation, and the second concerns the sentencing of Wilde to Reading Gaol to two years with hard labour in solitary confinement for committing acts of 'gross indecency'. The two come together in Nordau's assault on the 'degenerate' nature of Aesthetes: 'The ego-mania of decadentism, its love of the artificial, its aversion to nature, and to all forms of activity and movement, its megalomaniacal contempt for men and its exaggeration of the importance of art, have found their English representative among the "Aesthetes", the chief of whom is Oscar Wilde' (Nordau 1895, 317). This view was gaining widespread currency. Before Wilde's second trial, on 6 April 1895, the Tory *National Observer* remarked that there was 'not a man or woman in the English-speaking world possessed of the treasure of a wholesome mind who is not under a deep debt of gratitude to the Marquess of Queensberry for destroying the High Priest of the Decadents' (cited in Hyde 1973, 145).[1] Such contumely may well suggest that Decadence had by this point been established in the public's mind as a sexually perverse phenomenon. But, as Alan Sinfield forcefully argues, caution must be exercised when considering how and why Wilde's homosexual practices emerged as one of the most prominent aspects of Decadence. If Nordau's *Degeneration* attacked Wilde's mannered effeminacy, it had barely any interest in the Sins of the Cities of the Plain. Instead, as Sinfield sees it, the effeminate style that irritates Nordau 'correlates with degenerate leisure-class uselessness and its perverse ratification in aestheticism' (Sinfield 1994, 118). On this persuasive view, there was not, until the three trials had run their grisly course, an identifiable queer sterotype that Wilde could fulfil. Certainly, one could plausibly argue that the stigmatization of the 'queer' emerged from a longstanding and contentious debate about divergent styles of manly and effeminate masculinity. Yet the very thought that the Aesthete was by definition homosexual had not by the mid-1890s altogether come within cultural consciousness. Exactly the same might

---

[1] Hyde notes that 'it is possible that the article was written by Charles Whibley, but in any event Henley must take the responsibility for it'.

be said of the Decadents, as Symons first chose to style them in his essay of 1893.

There is no doubt that 'The Decadent Movement in Literature' has a striking perversity about it – in the broadest sense of this troublesome word. It may, first of all, seem odd indeed that an essay interested in 'moral and spiritual perversity' should have appeared in a family magazine: *Harper's New Monthly* with a massive circulation on both sides of the Atlantic. Indeed, as Laurel Brake suggests, the substance of Symons' contribution to this journal is 'hardly staid' in its description of the 'effeminate, over-civilized, deliberately abnormal' Des Esseintes, the arch-Aesthete of J.-K. Huysmans' *A Rebours* (Symons 1893, 862; Brake 1994, 118). Should we, then, assume that the editors of *Harper's* welcomed this kind of essay because it belonged to an older cultural formation that still believed that feature articles on literary coteries would act as a bulwark to the magazine's sense of cultural authority? Even if, as Brake says, this remains an open question, there is surely something apologetic about the advertisement for the November 1893 issue which announces the forthcoming publication of one of Pater's imaginary portraits in the same number as 'The Decadent Movement in Literature'. The advertisement states that 'Apollo in Picardy' is not ' "decadent" . . . in any proper sense, but rather poetically interpretative' (Brake 1994, 118).[2] Clearly the editors felt that some discretion had to be shown towards the term. But there are stranger things still about the content of Symons' essay itself.

Not only did he set about defining a term that he would eventually feel obliged to repudiate, Symons also drew within that definition a range of writers whose stylistic and political predilections would initially seem to be entirely incompatible with one another. His manner of itemizing the main features of literary Decadence unquestionably complies with the popular view of the 'sensational or lurid' 1890s that we have come to celebrate in the past hundred years. Each member of this movement, according to Symons, shares 'an intense self-consciousness, a restless curiosity in research, an oversubtilizing refinement upon refinement' (Symons 1893, 858). Yet when, in the closing paragraphs, Symons characterizes the work of Henley – the jingoistic Bard of Empire who also edited the *National Observer* – in exactly the same terms he uses to describe Paul Verlaine's work ('a disembodied voice, and yet the voice of a human soul' [Symons 1893, 862, 867]), then something has

---

2   The advertisement is reprinted in Brake 1994, 115.

gone awry. Puzzlingly, 'spiritual and moral perversity' either had an import that has long escaped our notice or it served as something of a malicious joke.[3] Little wonder, we might think, that Henley's name would disappear from *The Symbolist Movement in Literature*. But, then, so too did any allusion to Pater: the only other English writer whose works are detailed in the essay of 1893. Under Symons' initial understanding of Decadence, both authors were originally seen to be working towards similar ends: 'The prose of Mr Walter Pater, the verse of Mr Henley – to take two prominent examples – are attempts to do with the English language something of what Goncourt and Verlaine have done with French' (Symons 1893, 866). How, then, could Symons yoke together Pater's austere interest in that 'plenary substance' glimpsed only by 'one phase or facet' in a literary work (Pater 1913, 27) with the bombastic triumphalism of Henley's 'Invictus' (written in 1875) where the speaker pronounces: 'I am the master of my fate;/ I am the captain of my soul'. Henley's well-known poetic rallying-cry, as Jerome Hamilton Buckley puts it, 'grounds an activist philosophy on a personal Darwinism, a necessary faith in the survival of the biologically fit' (Buckley 1945, 65).[4] Nothing, given Henley's survivalist bravado, could appear more at odds with Paterian aestheticism.

Several critical responses have been made to Symons' selection of these unlikely bedfellows. In his pioneering study of literary transformations between 1880 and 1914, John A. Lester remarks that in this period 'one is confronted with unexpected connections between motifs which had seemed totally disparate'. Lester claims that this unhesitating juxtaposition of Henley and Pater shows how 'there was in fact a single underlying cultural crisis at work' (Lester 1968, xvii). But, disappointingly, he does not pursue the link between their names any further. Thornton, however, believes that Symons' judgement in this instance rests purely on a matter of stylistic correspondence: presumably the unconventional aspects of Henley's and Pater's works (Thornton 1983, 54–5). Yet when we look more closely at Symons' willingness to

---

[3] Remarking on how Symons' essay is a reply to a poem by Richard Le Gallienne that describes how the Decadent dreams 'of a new sin:/ An incest 'twixt the body and the soul' ('The Décadent to his Soul', *English Poems* [1892]), Thornton 'wonders with what maliciousness Symons chose – after a discussion of the Goncourts, Verlaine, Mallarmé, Maeterlinck, Villier de l'Isle Adam, and Huysmans – to represent Decadence in England by the work of Pater and W.E. Henley' (Thornton 1893, 23–24). Symons' selection of Pater, I would argue, is not exactly aberrant here.
[4] Buckley cites 'Invictus' on the same page.

commandeer Henley's poetry into the 'Decadent Movement', there is something more than the 'deformation' of style to be taken into account. It was not just Henley's virtuosic use of *vers libre* in some parts of his *In Hospital* sequence, first published in 1875, that Symons chose to accentuate. He was equally struck by the 'ache and throb of the body in its long nights on a tumbled bed' (Symons 1893, 867). In these innovative poems, which derive from the twenty months Henley spent in Joseph Lister's care at the Royal Edinburgh Infirmary, Henley's speaker recalls 'the thick, sweet mystery of chloroform' (Henley 1908, I 7). Symons would declare that such writing 'brought home to us as nothing else that I know in poetry has ever brought the physical sensations' (Symons 1893, 867). He had already elaborated Henley's attention to bodily feelings the previous year in the *Fortnightly Review*. Praising Henley's 'hymn to the ecstasy of conflict', 'The Song of the Sword' (1892), Symons declares that this poet 'is ashamed of none of the natural human instincts, and writes of women like a man, without effeminacy and without offence, content to be at one with the beneficent seasons, the will of nature' (Symons 1892, 189). Sensations, instincts, ecstasy – each word returns Symons to the physiological conditions of Henley's male protagonist, which other critics – such as Richard Le Gallienne – would regret as the imperialist poet's 'aggresively masculine stand' (Le Gallienne 1896, I 100). There is, then, a signal problem here. How can the Decadent male writer relish bodily impulses and yet 'write . . . about women like a man, without effeminacy'? If Des Esseintes proved to be the ultimate Decadent in his capacity for sensational experience, then it would appear to be the case that his pleasures accorded with an abnormal and effeminate temperament. The perceived oddity, therefore, in ranking Henley among the Decadents lies in how his work shares the '[e]laborately and deliberately perverse' features of the effeminate aesthete. So if the 'ache and throb of the body in its long nights on a tumbled bed' that we find in Henley's work is not effeminate', there must be something else that makes Henley' poetic representation of his hospital experiences closer than we might imagine to the rarefied world of Des Esseintes.

The only plausible connection between Henley and the Decadents lies in how the 'disembodied voice' makes itself heard, as Dowling suggests (Dowling 1986, 219–20). But in forging that link, we should not lose sight of perversity. Although this perverse aspect would ultimately be associated with the ignominy suffered by Wilde during the trials of 1895, the early conception of Decadence considered it in relation to the modernity of the male body. In 1892, after all, Symons was making a generous tribute to Henley's work when he declared that it was 'poetry made out of personal sensations, poetry which is half physiological, poetry which is pathology – yet essentially poetry' (Symons 1892, 186). The poem which complies most clearly with this view is 'Operation', which he cites in full. There Henley's hospitalized speaker recalls how 'the anaesthetic reaches/ Hot and subtle through your being' (Henley 1908, I 8–9). By refusing to write a complacent 'bourgeois' poetry that is 'aghast at passion, afraid of emotion, ashamed of frivolity' (Symons 1892, 188), Henley emerges for Symons as a wholly laudable figure who, in the tradition of Baudelaire, is developing 'a perverse, self-scrutinizing, troubled art of sensation and nerves' (Symons 1892, 184). It is only when, one year later, Symons repeats his appeal to the 'disembodied' condition of the Decadent 'voice' that we can begin to see the central tension between poetic representation and physical experience shared by the writers whom he groups together. For if, in this formulation, sensation is elevated on the one hand, it is also denied on the other. Implicitly, the male poet who writes of feelings remains in some respect alienated and at a distance from them. Yet this is obviously not the same as saying he is sexually perverted. Instead, Henley's description of anaesthesia has a close bearing on the forms of passivity, inutility, and states of intoxication that we would most readily associate not only with Des Esseintes, but also with the Decadent masculinity of a figure such as Lord Henry Wotton in Wilde's *The Picture of Dorian Gray* (1890, 1891).

In the 1890s, however, no one could be safely or stylistically perverse for long. It is well-known that in the early part of the decade perversion would become firmly associated with sexual pathology. According to the 1982 Supplement to the *OED*, the earliest use of the word in this context appears in Havelock Ellis' *Man and Woman* (1894). By the Edwardian period, the term had become a clinically standard one, notably in the earliest translations of Sigmund Freud's papers on hysteria. Thereafter, perversion was fully incorporated into popular sexology. My point is that Symons' essay of 1893 belongs to a specific moment when the notion of the perverse was decisively shifting from its stylistic to sexually pathological emphasis. Symons, of course, was hardly innocent of the sexual aspects to the perverse stylizations he sought to classify. But the significance of his appeal to the sexual style of this word assuredly lies in the paradox that many writers before him had apprehended in the perverse. The term rests on a long history of ideas – many of them theological – about deviating from the right path, suggesting that such deviation is necessitated by what in fact condemns it. In his persuasive genealogy of perversion. Jonathan Dollimore concludes that from the Middle Ages to the present, there has been an enduring 'paradox of perversion', since 'it is very often perceived as at once alien to what it threatens, and yet, mysteriously inherent within it' (Dollimore 1991, 121).[5] Dollimore's insight can enable us to see how the febrile and tormented male sexuality represented in the poetry of Symons is caught in a striking double bind: for its claim to normality as an unstoppable and compulsive force rests on the assumption that it is also alienated, excessive, morbid, unhealthy. In other words, these poems promulgate the view that male heteroeroticism is, so to speak, naturally perverse. And the most intriguing issue that emerges from Symons' absorption in perversity is that even those reviewers who treated his poetry with contempt would come to much the same conclusion. Such perversity, as those who disapproved of his work would admit, was perfectly comprehensible, even if it remained entirely unrespectable in a published poem. The harsh reception of his third collection, London Nights, helps to throw a good deal of light on the tension between sexual and stylistic perversity that made itself so powerfully manifest in 'The Decadent Movement in Literature'.

III

Appearing in late 1895, London Nights was Symons' most controversial work. From the outset, he encountered difficulties in securing a con-tract for his manuscript. The poet, John Davidson, submitted a luke-warm reader's report to the publisher of The Yellow Book, John Lane. 'Note always', writes Davidson, 'that the desire is utterly loveless and unimpassioned – mere and sheer libidinous desire' (Symons 1989, 109 n. 8). Finding a subsequent rejection by Heinemann 'inexplicable', Symons informed Edmund Gosse that he had turned to Selwyn Image

---

[5] Dollimore remarks that we 'do not find the explicitly sexual sense of perversion in the OED until its 1933 Supplement, and then only cautiously' (104). There is an additional point to be made about the link between the two substantival forms of perverse: perversion and perversity. Given that in the twentieth century, perversion has been utterly pathologized, sex radicals interested in fetishistic practices have often repudiated the term, choosing perversity instead: this question informs the titling of a special issue of New Formations 19 (1993), which indicates how troubling the idea of the sexually perverse remains in British and in American culture.

for advice about the contents of the volume. Image counselled him 'to omit nothing' on the 'ground of taste and morals', suggesting that it was 'the extremely *personal* note which has shocked people' (Symons 1989, 109). John Lane may have been singularly reluctant to publish *London Nights* because the poem by Symons he had showcased in the first issue of the *Yellow Book* had caused a furore in the press. More than any other contribution, Symons' 'Stella Maris' was found truly distasteful. Both the Cambridge magazine, *Granta*, and the London-based *Critic* poured scorn on this monologue about a chance encounter with a prostitute: to the latter, it ranked as nothing less than 'a poem of the gutter'. The Oxford journal, *Isis*, held a similar view, stating it was not clear why if Symons had 'on one occasion strayed from the path of virtue . . . he [should] take the public into his disgusting confidence' (cited in Mix 1969, 92–3). So by the time Leonard Smithers decided to publish *London Nights*, Symons' tarnished name elicited similar responses. The most provocative reaction came from the notoriously prurient *Pall Mall Gazette*, which wondered whether there might be 'other dirty-minded men who will regoice in the jungle that records the squalid and inexpensive amours of Mr Symons'. To this reviewer, this urban 'jungle' – a word emerging from the reigning imperialism of the day – reveals how Symons' life is 'more like a pig-sty' than the 'music-hall' he celebrates in many poems. Sentiments like these 'should bring him a joint-action for libel from every decent institution of the kind in London' (cited in Beckson 1987, 118–19). Such outrageous comments forced Symons to demand an apology from the editor.

In any case, Symons' interest in the music-halls – such as the Alhambra and the Empire in London, and La Moulin Rouge in Paris – was central to one of the most controversial debates about immorality in the mid-1890s. In London, a vigorous campaign was headed by Mrs Ormiston Chant to invoke repressive legislation that would stop prostitutes from plying their trade in the promenade marked off from the main auditorium of the Empire Theatre. The Empire, populated with female dancers and sex workers, symbolically fused eroticism and art. Addicted to the Empire, Symons would spend much of the decade writing enthusiastically about the female dancers whose physical presence was all too clearly a source of sexual excitement. But, as John Stokes has shown, the journalism that Symons produced on the music-halls for journals such as the *Sketch* and the *Savoy* 'often veers between these two poles: tolerance of natural proclivities and admiration for artistic expertise' (Stokes 1989, 61). At times, he was utterly disingenuous in his defence of the Empire. 'I have visited the Empire of average about once a week in my function as critic for several newspapers', wrote Symons in the *Pall Mall Gazette*, 'and I must say that whenever I've had occasion to stand in the promenade I have never in a single instance been accosted by a women'. The theatre in question, he argued, was a 'place of entertainment, the most genuinely artistic and the most absolutely unobjectionable that I know in any country' (cited in Stokes 1989, 60, and Beckson 1987, 110). Yet the poems in *London Nights*, of course, tell a rather different story about how the music-hall unleashed his raging desires.

Opposition to Symons' poems reveals that the hydraulic nature of male sexuality was hardly surprising in itself. In the *National Observer*, it is clear that Symons' desires are far from incomprehensible. Instead, the reviewer is provoked by the idea that commonplace sexual experience should have been permitted to pass into discourse:

> Our chief marvel in reading Mr Arthur Symons' *London Nights* was that a respectable publisher should have been willing to abet him in the production of such dreary indecencies. We have no intention in wasting many words over a most disagreeable volume. It is given to a majority of mankind at one time or another to have some such experience as Mr Symons describes, but for the most part, thank heaven! they do not gloat over them, and roll them on the tongue, and write about them in a style which recalls the cold-blooded catalogues of a semi-educated house-agent. Let any impartial person read – if he can for very nausea – the poem called 'Liber Amoris', which seems to contain the sum and substance of Mr Symons' erotic evangel, and witness if we lie. (Anon 1895, 717)

In 'Liber Amoris' – the tenth poem in a sequence dedicated to a ballet-dancer under the name of Bianca – the male speaker declares how 'long ago' he 'loved good women'. But not until he has encountered the 'sterile and mysterious bliss' of Bianca's 'voluptuous presence' was he fully satisfied. In rather jolting couplets, he explores how the woman's experience, like his own, is subject to 'the aching sense of sex' which 'Wholly controls' the 'shaken currents' of her 'blood' (Symons 1924, 265–8). Although these brief extracts clearly indicate the frankness of Symons' appeal to the cravings of the flesh, and his specific interest in an active and responsive female sexuality, it should not be thought it was simply his representation of male heteroeroticism that wearied the *National Observer*. To be open about wholly understandable sexual experiences was to violate codes of respectability, and to appear only semi-educated. Needless to say, class condescension of this kind indicates that the imagined world of the house-agent lay in dangerous proximity to that of the cultured poet. Yet curiously, this point is borne out by the subject-matter we find in some of Henley's best-known poems.

Henley's *London Voluntaries* (1893) – with their militaristic titling – enshrined for Symons all that was modern in English poetry. 'Here, at last', writes Symons, 'is a poet who can so enlarge the limits of his verse as to take in London'. And he goes on to add: 'I think that might be the test of poetry which professes to be modern – its capacity for dealing with London, with what one sees or might see there, indoors and out' (Symons 1892, 184). In fact, one feature of these largely exuberant 'voluntaries' that praise the metropolitan landscape is their attention to sexual energy. The fifth poem, for example, reveals London as part of a sexualized pastoral where 'spring clouds' bear their weight like 'matrons heavy and aglow'. No wonder that 'Milk' pours 'from the wild breasts of the wilful Day', as 'this freshet of desire' passes down Piccadilly (Henley 1908, II 93). 'Certainly', writes William B. Thesing, 'Henley's buxom and active matrons display no signs of the sexual sterility or neuroses that would afflict Eliot's urban dwellers a generation later' (Thesing 1982, 185). To some extent, this observation is accurate. Henley was not in any respect averse to the idea of 'sex' – as eroticism was increasingly named. Indeed, it struck Henley as central to literary creativity. Writing in the *Athenaeum*, for example, Henley would praise how George Meredith 'has considered sex – the great subject, the leaven of imaginative art' (Henley 1908, V 50). But the drift of *London Voluntaries* is not quite as wholesome in its eroticism as Thesing might lead us to believe. Even if this universe of fecund desire witnesses the 'sacred impulse of the May/ Brightening like sex made sunshine' through every woman's 'veins', it is still the case that the life-force animating this urban world remains a 'lewd, perennial, overmastering spell' (Henley 1908, V 94, 97). This 'genial wave' is ultimately 'Wanton and wondrous'. Such phrasing suggests that, far from coming from noble origins, the power of sex resides in qualities that might be thought of as impure, if not immoral. In other words, even when this avowedly Tory poet sought to write of the glory of sex, his choice of vocabulary could not but suggest that in the metropolis desire came from sources that were irremediably tainted. The buxom matron may appear at the other end of the spectrum from the pernicious harlot in Henley's fourth 'voluntary'. Both, however, belong to a circuit in which 'no woman but disdains . . . / To vail [i.e. display] the ensigns of her womanhood' (Henley 1908, V 94). In London, whether among madonnas or magdalens, there is no escape from what Henley oddly words as the 'insolent and comely stream/ Of appetence' (Henley 1908, V 93). It is almost as if there is something rude in the erotic awakening of the male speaker who, making his way through the crowds, experiences his attraction to one woman after another. Yet there is enough joy beating in 'the enormous heart of London' to conceal the coarsening aspect to this 'genial wave' that energizes this metroplitan scene. The point is that, even for the healthy advocate of manliness, eroticism – no matter how 'comely' in its charms – has a fundamentally tainted source, and Symons' poems emphasize its degraded and degrading origins over and over again.

On the face of it, 'Stella Maris' – the poem that gained Symons greatest notoriety – could not be more dissimilar in style from *London Voluntaries*. Where Henley's confident striding lines have a Whitmanian magnanimity about them, Symons' poem, by contrast, takes its guiding influence from Pre-Raphaelite sources that tend towards the gothic and the pagan. But that should not obscure the 'lewd' and 'wanton' premise upon which both writers consider sex. In many ways, it has proved difficult to establish this view because the critical revolt against 'Stella Maris' reactivated the assault that Dante Gabriel Rossetti had experienced at the hands of Robert Buchanan in the 'The Fleshly School of Poetry' (1871). Among the pieces Rossetti included in his offending volume, *Poems* (1870), was 'Jenny', an interior monologue that gives voice to a scholarly young man's thoughts about a night he has spent dancing with a prostitute. Elsewhere, I have written on Rossetti's cautious revision of his poem to ensure that neither mention of sex nor conversation between Jenny and her client could be heard – lest the work was condemned outright (Bristow 1993). Instead, Rossetti's persona wracks his conscience, as he muses on his fearful fascination with the prostitute's beautiful yet sexually contaminated body. In any case, 'Stella Maris' is modelled on Rossetti's monologue, not only in terms of its subject-matter, but also in its unevenly patterned couplets. Symons' awkward tetrameters follow Rossetti's lead in exploiting enjambment to loosen the troubled modulations of the speaker's thoughts. Like 'Jenny', much of 'Stella Maris' develops an intervolved syntax that culminates in questions. But where Rossetti's poem constantly draws the speaker back into deliberations about the moral status of prostitution, 'Stella Maris' grapples with the memory of sex. Having been approached by a prostitute, Symons' speaker gradually realizes that he has slept with her before, and he wonders why she –

more than any of the other women he has paid for sexual services –
should cause him to reflect on the deal they are about to strike:

> I too have sought on many a breast
> The ecstasy of love's unrest,
> I too have had my dreams, and met
> (Ah me!) how many a Juliet.
> Why is it, then, that I recall
> You, neither first nor last of all?

Rather than turning into another of his 'chance romances of the
streets', this female figure haunts him like a ghost. At first imagined as
a 'Nereid' romantically draped in seaweed, then figured as a 'wraith',
she advances like a *femme fatale* along the 'shadowy shore', goddess and
demon in one. Gothic in the extreme, this environment intensifies his
recollection of how they were once united 'In the intolerable, the
whole/ Rapture of the embodied soul'. Yet this phantasmal world
threatens to undo the fantasy he seeks to weave around her. For he
knows how 'that ineffable delight' probably has no meaning whatsoever
to the woman he sacriligiously names Stella Maris: 'What shall it profit
me to know,/ Your heart holds many a Romeo?' (Symons 1924, I 203–5).
Repeated twice, this question probes the speaker's unease with the
alienating effects of sexual commodification. But 'Stella Maris' is hardly
unique among Symons' poems in representing a man's sexual experience at odds with itself. *London Nights* often suggests that male sexuality
is irredeemably – and thus perhaps necessarily – in a state of alienation,
not least from the body of a woman.

Throughout this collection, Symons' speaker locates the intensity of
sexual desire in pathological terms: morbid, sterile, shivering, fainting.
The first poem in the sequence entitled 'Bianca' provides the best
example of how the female body is supposed to figure this perversity.
Almost every stanza focuses on one part of her fascinating flesh: cheek,
eyes, mouth, hands, and lips. This technique – which some would claim
characterizes the dehumanizing tendencies of modern pornography –
interweaves with the spectral gothic touches that we find in 'Stella
Maris'. But the impulse to anatomize the female body fails to produce
the intensities that would seem to inform this desire. The more he
fetishizes each bodily part, the more her flesh dissolves before him.
Relishing the 'morbid faintness' of Bianca's pale complexion, he observes that no sooner has he kissed her than her lips 'close/ Into a false
and phantom rose'. Her deathly physiology comes most clearly into
view at the moment she reaches orgasm:

Through her closed lips that cling to mine,
Her hands that hold me and entwine
Her body that abandoned lies,
Rigid with sterile ecstasies,
A shiver knits her flesh to mine.   (Symons 1925, I 255)

In the expressly loose syntax – where the clauses feel somewhat disas-sociated because of the long delayed main verb – the moment of sexual pleasure undergoes a form of grammatical dissolution. Physical close-ness meets with emotional division. All that is left of their union is the abandonment, rigidity, sterility, and sensational shivering of her pallid body. Not for one moment do we see a flicker of romantic love. But, then, the general tendency of these poems is to withdraw from affective attachment: to make sexual intercourse, in other words, as impersonal as possible. In 'Rosa Mundi', for example, a 'pale angel' advises the male speaker to choose 'a delicate Lust' rather than an ideal 'Love' whose 'infinity' is 'Ever a longing in vain/ After a vanishing goal' (Symons 1924, I 202, 201).

The repudiation of romantic love marks the perversity of Symons' poetry. This represents, I would claim, a distinctly modern under-standing of human sexuality as a type of pathology, connected with physiological impulses that are in some respect diseased. The word that most powerfully concentrates this feature of 'Bianca' is 'sterile'. Not only does this epithet connote the hospitalized world that fascinated Symons in Henley's stylistically innovative poetry, it also points to the non-reproductive function of sexual pleasure. Yet more to the point, the adjective lays greatest emphasis on the woman's body as the site of these pathological perceptions of eroticism. To be sure, the perversity of Symons' appeal to 'sterile ecstasies' rests on a well-established en-semble of images and representations of the Victorian prostitute, a frequently demonized figure who most clearly forced the troubling link between sexuality and impurity. But it would be misleading to revert Symons' writing to the heritage of Victorian moralism that he was seeking to resist. His speaker hardly sets out to condemn the ballet-girl whose 'phantom rose' blushes from her 'thirsting lips'. Instead, true to his Decadent precepts, he is claiming that this is the natural condition of sexuality, a type of sensational illness over which a man has no control, and which can legitimately remain 'sterile' in its pleasures. Such infertile joys render male heteroeroticism unapologetically – if not naturally – shameful.

Yet even if the speaker's encounter with Bianca is not subject to

Victorian moralistic treatment, she is a decidedly traditional figuration upon which the man projects his desire, speaks his soul, and yet remains a 'disembodied voice'. Just as in Rossetti's 'Jenny', the man's own physicality hardly emerges in anything like the detail accorded to the woman's flesh. Repeatedly, the female body acts as a screen on which Symons' male persona witnesses the perverse patternings of what he wants to possess. In 'La Mélinite: Moulin Rouge', for instance, the dancer who captivates him exudes a repeatedly 'morbid grace', as she performs before a mirror in a 'dance of shadows' among atmospheric 'orange-rosy lamps' (Symons 1924, I 190). The female dancer iconizes for him pagan forces that puritans and moralists had done their utmost to purge from modern society. That, at least, was the view Symons advanced in 'The World as Ballet' (1898):

> The dance is life, animal life, having its own way passionately. Part of that natural madness which men were once wise enough to include in religion, it began with the worship of disturbing deities, the gods of ecstasy, for whom wantonness, and wine, and all things in which energy passes into an ideal excess, were sacred. It was cast out when religion cast out nature: for, like nature itself, it is a thing of evil to those who renounce instincts. From the first it has mimed the instincts. (Symons 1924, IX 244)

Yet no matter how much Symons would idealize the animalistic and ritualized instincts brought to life by the dancers he frequently met at the Alhambra and the Empire, he would find it hard in his poetry to establish the pronouncedly masculine component of this febrile sexuality. For the 'disembodied voice' would lead his male speakers away from the 'natural madness' that they were trying to approach through stylistic perversity. The more we analyze these poems, the clearer it becomes that the dancer fascinates Symons precisely because she embodies a sexuality that his tormented speakers cannot themselves express.

The male body forever eludes representation in *London Nights*, even if it is subject time and again to sensational frissons. In his tribute 'To a Dancer', Symons' persona sits among the busy audience of a music-hall, sensing that at every turn the performer gazes at him alone. Even though he feels a 'quickening fire within', it is her physical presence which amplifies the specifically Decadent interest in erotic sensation: 'Her body's melody,/ In silent waves of wandering sounds/ Thrills to the sense of all around'. Like La Mélinite before the mirror, this dancer has the prerogative to express a 'desire that leaps' to the man's 'desire'. All he can do is watch while her dance affects him 'intoxicatingly' (Symons 1924, I 171). It might, then, be said that the male spectator is strikingly passive in this situation. The woman dances, the man responds. And while she sexualizes the body, he becomes increasingly disembodied, as the intoxication of her performance works its heady effect upon him. The first stanza of the jaunty 'Prologue' to *London Nights* endorses this view. There the speaker finds himself frustrated because he cannot move like the dancers on the stage:

> My life is like a music-hall,
> Where, in the impotence of rage,
> Chained by enchantment to my stall,
> I see myself upon the stage
> Dance to amuse a music-hall.

But his frustration will not confine him altogether. Rather than remain stuck in his seat, he hallucinates how he might perform: 'It is my very self I see/ Across the cloudy cigarette'. He has, in other words, imagined himself dancing on the stage. True to the artificiality that Symons relished in this theatrical context, his speaker's self-projection is 'Painted' and 'pathetically gay'. He can hardly believe he is 'this thing that turns and trips', in the manner of the female dancers (Symons 1924, I 170). Only by adopting a 'disembodied voice' can this Decadent poet confront a man with an image of his own physical desires. Unable to have the dancer, he wishes to be one himself.

And there, I think, rests the chief difficulty in Symons' model of sexual perversity: it leaves the Decadent poet confronted with himself – and not a female dancer – as the object of his desire. Estranged from the flesh, he yearns to flit across the stage only to vanish into darkness like Bianca or La Mélinite. So it turns out that the dancer and the prostitute, while embodying carnality, are forever evanescing among the 'dance of shadows' that tantalize the man's projection of what he might himself become. This 'Prologue', therefore, discloses how Symons' female figures represent a femininity that his poetic persona wishes to represent, not just for himself, but as himself. In the light of this interpretation, one might therefore infer that both 'Stella Maris' and 'Bianca' manifest the 'disembodied voice' of a man who seeks to occupy the body of a woman, so strong is his identification to be her. And since women are so closely identified with the body, while the Decadent male experiences sensations that disembody him, then it is not so surprising that he finds himself thwarted by the 'impotence of

rage'. At once sensational and immobilized, the man in the stalls of the
music-hall articulates his envy towards the bodily movement of those
women whom he regards as the ultimate icons of sexuality. Spectator
and spectacle in one, his desire travels rapidly back and forth between
'impotence' and 'rage', stasis and movement, and – most crucially –
masculinity and femininity.

Symons' dancers have not, to my knowledge, been read in this
manner before.[6] Instead, they have been given plenty of attention
because they form part of a significant dialogue with the greater poet,
W.B. Yeats, and their impact on literary modernism. Through the
Rhymers Club, Symons' contact with Yeats would encourage a move
from a celebration of the music-hall to larger cultural concerns. Even
if, as Ian Fletcher observes, it remains difficult to prove that Yeats was
influenced by Symons' innumerable poems about dancers, we can see
in works such as 'Dance of the Daughters of Herodias' (1897) 'an
ambitious attempt to present the Dance as a composite image: of the
poet's situation; of the predicament of a society which had rejected his
wisdom; of the dancer as at once fascinating and terrible; warning and
epiphany at once' (Fletcher 1987, 262–3).[7] So in Yeats's 'Nineteen
Hundred and Nineteen' (1928) the dance has become the most potent
figuration of cultural apocalypse: 'A sudden blast of dusty wind and
after/ Thunder of feet, tumult of images' (Yeats 1990, 256). But although there is no doubt that Symons' escapades with dancers in the
mid-1890s had significant bearings on the development of Yeats's
mysticism, this piece of literary history tends to omit that Symons wrote
ceaselessly about the female performer as an emblem of perverse desire.
If it is the case, as Fletcher suggests, that some of the roots of literary
modernism are to be traced to Symons' poetry, then Bianca, La
Mélinite, and the many other dancers inhabiting *London Nights* need
to be considered for the erotic legacy that Decadence left not only to
Yeats, but also to T.S. Eliot. Certainly, one of the main heirs to Symons'
perversity is 'The Love Song of J. Alfred Prufrock' (1919). In that poem,
as Maud Ellmann vividly puts it, 'the female body unravels into an
inventory of parts' in a poem which subjects its whole environment to
the 'phantasmal amputations of synecdoche' (Ellmann 1987, 78). To
be sure, the female hands, faces, and voices – not to say 'arms . . ./Arms
that are braceleted and white and bare' – that we glimpse in Eliot's

---

[6] Little critical attention has been given to these poems. An exception is
Gordon.
[7] Fletcher's discussion should be compared with Kermode's.

monologue accentuate the disfigurations of male heterosexuality in its most alienated modernist guise. While Prufrock stares at the evening like 'a patient etherised upon a table' (Eliot 1974, 15, 13), there is the flickering memory of a 'disembodied' Decadence where literary masculinity was increasingly ill-at-ease with itself. Such unease comes most prominently – and troublingly – into view in Symons' later reflections on the heyday of literary Decadence.

IV

Much later in life, Symons wrote a number of retrospective accounts about his nights of passion with various female dancers from the music-halls when Decadence was in its most perverse element. In fact, one unpublished memoir of La Mélinite is little more than a transcription into prose of the poem entitled 'Bianca'. Given that Symons' biographer, Karl Beckson, identifies Bianca as the nineteen-year-old Lydia with whom Symons had a torrid affair in 1893, the interchangeability of the content of the poem dedicated to her with the memoir about La Mélinite – entitled 'Marcelle and Other Parisian Diversions' – may well say a great deal about the uniformity of his sexual experiences:

> At times, she hardly breathed, she trembled all over, shivered, shuddered: rained her kisses on men as she embraced me: her mouth on mine that ached with heat. Then her hands seized my hands, she strained them as her lips sucked at my lips. Then, as they closed inextricably, her abandoned body that was abandoned to mine became rigid with sterile ecstasies. (Symons 1977, 146–7)[8]

But here the 'sterile ecstasies' become more precisely figured than in 'Bianca' once we discover that La Mélinite was a 'Lesbian' who had an 'almost cruel passion for men'. Like one of Baudelaire's *femmes damnées* in *Les fleurs du mal* (1857), the perverse passion of this 'Lesbian' appears to be based on her complete separation from reproductive femininity. Her 'sterility' defines the intensity of her difference from other women: she embodies a violent sensuality that runs against the grain of each and every naturalized assumption about Victorian womanhood. The

---

8   No date is given for this memoir.

'Lesbian', then, enshrines the most alienated and thus erotic form of sexuality.

Much the same might be said for Lydia. In a separate memoir, dating from 1920, Symons turns once again to an identical repertoire of terms to celebrate her 'almost shamelessly animal' passion. Here, too, he connects the eroticism with depravity, evil, and malice. In one paragraph after another, similar epithets stream out: 'Feverish, fatal, she was the most unholy mixture of complex propensities, or enigmatic surprises and surmises, of infinite perversities'. Indeed, her 'indescribable and passionate curiosity . . . was perverse'. 'I made her', he triumphantly declares, 'perverse' (Symons 1977, 157, 162, 163).[9] But even if the interminable recurrence to this word has by now made it clear what Symons thought of his sexuality, another of his memoirs indicates that his perversity had a heterosexual privilege.

In 'Sex and Aversion', written after his mental breakdown in 1909, Symons made one statement that confirmed what everyone had felt about him all along: 'Sex – the infernal fascination of Sex – even before I actually realized the meaning of its stirrings in me – has been my chief obsession'. Spontaneous desire drives to the very core of his creative being. 'Without the possession of women', he asks, 'how can one create?' Yet once this somewhat ambiguous declaration has been made (since it is not clear whether he feels he must possess women or be possessed by them), he quickly launches into a violent attack on those male critics and artists in whom he discerns a 'kind of sterilization'. G.F. Watts, John Ruskin, and Thomas Carlyle all come under the same rubric of the 'sexless' writer – the latter perhaps because of frequently circulated rumours about his impotence. Yet by far the worst offender in Symons' mind is the man who was reviled as the 'High Priest of the Decadents':

Wilde's vices were not simply intellectual perversions, they were physiological. This miserable man had always been under the influence of one of those sexual inversions which turned him into a kind of Hermaphroditus. That distress which he tried to express in his writings after his condemnation had nothing virile in it; and his best known tragedy *Salome* reveals in its perversion of a legend his own sexual perversion. As he grew older the womanish side of him grew more and more evident. Lautrec saw him in Paris, and in the appalling portrait of him he shows Wilde, swollen, puffed out,

9   Beckson dates this memoir from 1920 (Beckson 1987, 100).

bloated and sinister. The form of the mouth which he gave him is more than any thing exceptional; no such mouth ought ever to have existed: it is a woman's that no man who is normal could ever have had. (Symons 1977, 146–47)[10]

This homophobic outburst shows how the pathology of male sexuality has gone too far. And for one good reason: Wilde has been transformed into a gross parody of nothing less than a dancing-girl. It is, after all, hardly insignificant that Symons sees how Toulouse Lautrec pays attention to Wilde's 'woman's' mouth. No other painter can rival Lautrec's fame for representing the exciting world of La Moulin Rouge that captivated Symons. In assenting to the widespread sexological view that homosexual desire was embodied by the invert, Symons is forced up against the impossible recognition that his love of the perverse cannot in any respect be, so to speak, a perversion. Even Wilde's Decadent drama that influenced Symons' powerful poem on the Daughters of Herodias ultimately figures an unacceptable sexual identity: for it shows a man who had forsaken his virility for the sexualized body of a *femme fatale*.

Yet we need to look twice at this wholehearted repudiation of Wilde: for Symons is attempting to stigmatize the 'High Priest of the Decadents' precisely because Wilde was thought to have embodied his perversity in nothing less than a demonic female dancer whose own furious footsteps make such an impression on Symons' work. So if Wilde's perversion emerges most forcefully through the figure of Salomé, it needs to be borne in mind that Symons also wished to 'trip' and 'turn' like a dancer as he sat transfixed at the music-hall. This memoir, then, does more than simply return us to the all too familiar picture of the 1890s where a lurid, sensational, and effeminate homosexuality characterizes Decadence. Instead, the intensity of Symons' repudiation of the 'bestial', 'ruined', and 'ravaged' Wilde accentuates the ambivalent status of the Decadent terms upon which he sought to claim the 'natural madness' of sexual perversity. Initially, it was in the 'moral and spiritual perversity' of the time that Symons could find the expression of physiological sensation and pathological conditions as the very essence of the Decadent moment. But, after the trials of 1895, categories of gender would become overlaid on the previously libertine impulses that characterized the leisure-class connoisseurship of Des Esseintes. And so the effeminate pervert and the virile pervert had to

10 No date is given for this memoir.

part company – not least perhaps because of their proximity. Maybe in Wilde's seemingly womanish guise, Symons witnessed the spectre of his own conflicted 'possession' of women.

The matter, however, cannot simply rest there. Symons never quite resolved the problem of perversity that he had opened up in 1893. Other later writings reveal how difficult it proved for him to compre-hend male homosexuality, since yet again same-sex desire was assuredly on a broad continuum with the perversity that defined Symons' own heterosexual compulsions. Writing on John Addington Symonds in the liberal *Fortnightly Review* in 1924, for example, he discreetly alluded to the open secret of this man's homophilia, the details of which were at that time preserved in Symonds' unpublished memoirs. (So sensitive did Symonds' family regard these materials that once the manuscript had been deposited in the London Library in 1926, a fifty-year ban was placed on their publication.) 'It seems evident', writes Symons, 'from all we know of him, and from all we have read of him that Symonds was very sexual; that he was to a certain extent abnormal; that those morbid and neurotic strains in his vigorous personality become more obvious year by year'. But there was, at least, one saving grace: 'He knew himself to be, neither finally nor fatally, an *homo duplex*' (Symons 1977, 120) – by which, I take it, he means an invert. Equally inscrutable was Herbert Horne. In 'A Study in Morbidity', Symons would observe how Horne was 'sexually endowed to an excess which was morbid'. But here, too, the sex drive of a homosexual critic forced Symons to hesitate when it came to considering the 'aching *sterility*' of such types: it 'may or may not make them barren of success' (Symons 1977, 127–8).[11] In each instance, the man-loving man displays all those signs of erotic exces-siveness and morbidity that Symons at one time readily associated with the natural perversity of his own heteroerotic encounters.

Ultimately, Symons' essays, poems, and memoirs force us to see how precarious were the 'sterile ecstasies' of literary Decadence. For what establishes the 'natural madness' of sexual desire in these works is what equally makes it into a perplexingly unnatural thing. The trouble, of course, in traditional accounts of the 1890s is that male homosexuality has supposedly provided an answer for the 'lurid and sensational' overtones of the period. If that legend is perpetuated, then it will remain difficult to see how Decadence might be equally defined by a general perversity of male sexuality: one in which a man's fantasy of becoming

---

[11] No date is given for this memoir.

a female dancer could act as an apparent sign of his identification either to have or to be a woman. That Symons felt an unbearable cultural pressure to force such a violent separation between the two has, I think, much to tell us about how and why the twentieth century quickly absorbed the seeming stability proferred by the hetero/homo binary divide. This divide has assuredly masked the proximity that Symons first perceived between the 'disembodied voice[s]' of those diverse writers who supposedly shared the momentary perversity of Decadence: a movement which, by definition, announced that a period of literary – if not cultural – history had decisively come to an end.

Works Cited

Anon., 1895. *National Observer*, 2 November, 717.

Beckson, Karl, 1987. *Arthur Symons: A Life*, Oxford: Clarendon Press.

Brake, Laurel, 1994. *Subjugated Knowledges: Journalism, Gender and Literature in the Nineteenth Century*, Basingstoke: Macmillan.

Bristow, Joseph, 1993. ' "What If To Her All This Were Said?": Dante Gabriel Rossetti and the Silencing of "Jenny" ', in Nigel Smith, ed. *Essays and Studies: Literature and Censorship*, Cambridge: D.S. Brewer, 96–117.

Buckley, Jerome Hamilton, 1945. *William Ernest Henley: A Study in the 'Counter-Decadence' of the Nineties*, Princeton, NJ: Princeton University Press.

Crackanthorpe, Hubert, 1894. 'Reticence in Literature: Some Roundabout Remarks', *The Yellow Book*, 2, 259–69.

Dollimore, Jonathan, 1991. *Sexual Dissidence: Augustine to Wilde, Freud to Foucault*, Oxford: Clarendon Press.

Dowling, Linda C, 1986. *Language and Decadence in the Victorian Fin de Siècle*, Princeton, NJ: Princeton University Press.

Eliot, T.S., 1974. *Collected Poems, 1909–1962*, London: Faber.

Ellmann, Maud, 1987. *The Poetics of Impersonality: T.S. Eliot and Ezra Pound*, Brighton: Harvester Press.

Fletcher, Ian, 1987. *W.B. Yeats and His Contemporaries*, Brighton: Harvester Press.

Gordon, Jan B., 1971. 'The Danse Macabre of Arthur Symons' *London Nights*', *Victorian Poetry*, 9, 429–43.

Henley, W.E., 1908. *The Works of W.E. Henley*, 7 vols, London: David Nutt.

Hyde, H. Montgomery, 1973. *The Trials of Oscar Wilde*, second edition, New York: Dover.

Kermode, Frank, 1957. *The Romantic Image*. London: Routledge.

Le Gallienne, Richard, 1896. *Retrospective Reviews: A Literary Log*, 2 vols, London: John Lane.

Lester, John A., Jr., 1968. *Journey through Despair 1880–1914: Transformations in British Literary Culture*, Princeton, NJ: Princeton University Press.

Mix, Katherine Lyon, 1969. *A Study in Yellow: The Yellow Book and Its Contributors*, New York: Greenwood Press.

Nordau, Max, 1895. *Degeneration*, second edition, trans. Anon., London: Heinemann.

Pater, Walter, 1913. *Appreciations with An Essay on Style*, London: Macmillan.

——, 1921. *Marius the Epicurean: His Sensations and Ideas*, 2 vols, London: Macmillan.

Sinfield, Alan, 1994. *The Wilde Century: Effeminacy, Oscar Wilde and the Queer Moment*, London: Cassell.

Stokes, John, 1989. *In the Nineties*, Hemel Hempstead: Harvester-Wheatsheaf.

Symons, Arthur, 1892. 'Mr Henley's Poetry', *Fortnightly Review*, NS 52, 183–92.

——, 1893. 'The Decadent Movement in Literature', *Harper's New Monthly Magazine* 87, 858–67.

——, 1896. 'Editorial Note', *Savoy* 1.

——, 1924. 'A Study of John Addington Symonds', *Fortnightly Review*, NS 115, 228–39.

——, 1924. *Studies in Two Literatures*, London: Martin Secker.

——, 1977. *The Memoirs of Arthur Symons*, ed. Karl Beckson, University Park, PA: Pennsylvania State University Press.

——, 1989. *Selected Letters, 1880–1935*, ed. Karl Beckson and John M. Munro, Basingstoke: Macmillan.

Thesing, William B., *The London Muse: Victorian Poetic Responses to the City*, Athens, GA: University of Georgia Press.

Thornton, R.K.R., 1983. *The Decadent Dilemma*, London: Edward Arnold.

Yeats, W.B., 1990. *The Poems*, ed. Daniel Albright, London: Dent.

Feminism and the End of Eras: Apocalypse and Utopia

MARGARET BEETHAM

Rousseau exerts himself to prove that all *was* right originally: a crowd of authors that all *is* now right: and I, that all will *be* right.
Mary Wollstonecraft, 1975, A *Vindication of the Rights of Woman*, (1792), Penguin, p. 95

And I dreamed a dream.
I dreamed I saw a land. And on the hills walked brave women and brave men, hand in hand. And they looked into each other's eyes, and they were not afraid.
And I saw the women also held each other's hands.
And I said to him beside me, 'What place is this?'
And he said, 'This is heaven.'
And I said, 'Where is it?'
And he answered, 'On earth.'
And I said, 'When shall these things be?'
And he answered, 'IN THE FUTURE.'
Olive Schreiner, 1894, 'Three Dreams in a Desert', *Dreams* (1890), Roberts Brothers, p. 84

By the late twentieth century, our time, a mythic time, we were all chimeras, theorised and fabricated hybrids of machine and organism, in short, we were cyborgs . . . The Cyborg is a condensed image of both imagination and material reality, the two joined centres struc-turing any possibility of historical transformation . . . This [manifesto] is an argument for *pleasure* in the confusion of boundaries and for *responsibility* in their construction. It is also an effort to contribute to socialist-feminist culture and theory in a post-modernist, non-naturalist mode and in the utopian tradition of imagining a world without gender, which is a world without genesis, and maybe also a world without end.
Donna Haraway, 1991, 'A Cyborg Manifesto', *Simians, Cyborgs and Women; the Reinvention of Nature*, p. 150

Acknowledgements. My thanks to Janet Batsleer, who read this in draft and helped to clarify my thinking; to Erica Burman, who gave me her unpublished aticle on false memory syndrome to read and sent me back to Walter Benjamin; to Karen Hunt, who allowed me to read a chapter of her forthcom-ing book, *Equivocal Feminists; the S.D.F. and the Woman Question* (Cambridge, 1996). All are involved with me in the utopian project of Women's Studies.

I. *The Idea of the Millennium*

THE JUDEO-CHRISTIAN UNDERSTANDING of history as a narrative with a beginning, a middle and an end still powerfully shapes the Western European/American imagination and politics (Kermode 1966).[1] The idea of the millennium persists into late twentieth-century secular culture as evidence of its power. In eschatology, the Judeo-Christian theory and narrative of The End, the apocalyptic and the utopian have always been intertwined. The Four Horsemen and the Angels of Destruction in the Book of Revelation herald the wiping away of all tears, the descent of the New Jerusalem from Heaven to Earth, adorned like a bride for her husband (Revelation 21, 3-4).

At the centre of this narrative, therefore, is desire, imaged as both social and erotic, a longing for the restoration of lost community and for the beloved. This image of the 'beloved community' persisted into Western European millenarianism. According to its most notable exponent, Norman Cohn, millenarians always pictured The End as a historical transformation which would be 'collective . . ., terrestrial . . ., imminent . . ., total . . . and miraculous' (Cohn 1970, 13).

Approaching the end of the second Christian millennium, we seem to be living indeed in a mythic time, a time beyond the endings, after history, beyond the reach of grand narratives, post- everything; -modernism, -feminism and, of course, post-Marxism, that most important modern version of the narrative of historical transformation. Despite the triumphalism which greeted this ending, it is the apocalyptic rather than the utopian which dominates the stories we tell ourselves. Taking down the Berlin Wall and toppling Lenin from his pedestal have not brought the material and emotional satisfactions they seemed to promise.

In Britain concern for the economic and social manifests itself in anxiety about the future of 'The Family' an institution predicated on the heterosexual couple who socialise children into a proper femininity and – even more importantly – a proper masculinity. The apocalyptic discourses which surround Aids make explicit what is everywhere implicit, that anxieties about gender and sexuality pervade our end-of-the century narratives. Ironically it is from within the gay community

---

[1] I locate myself and the debates I discuss here within this Western European/American and specifically British context.

that the death-bringing 'Angels in America' have been redeemed for creativity and the wiping away of tears (Kushner 1992).

Feminism, which as a politics and a discourse has made these issues central to its project, has had its own end-of-the-century crisis. Politically fragmented, theoretically and institutionally under attack – both from conservatives and radicals – feminism seems to be stumbling towards apocalypse rather than looking towards utopia. Yet, in as far as it has centred on a narrative of historical transformation and liberation, feminism has historically been utopian. Ever since Mary Wollstonecraft, feminists have offered a critique of their present society, its myths of origin and its narrative resolutions. But they have also argued that if it 'remains *simply* reactive, *merely* a critique, [it] . . . remains on the very grounds it wishes to question and transform' (Grosz 1992, 360).

The commitment to a future not yet visible but characterised by an utterly new politics and poetic has therefore united feminists from very different perspectives. This utopianism always threatens to disrupt existing norms. It refuses existing categories – specifically those of 'masculine' and 'feminine' – and reconfigures desire in an excess which is marked by an eruption into italics or capitals in each of the quotations of my epigraphs. At the centre of modern 'progress', that storm blowing from Paradise, as Walter Benjamin described it, feminists have offered their own vision of the desirable ending (Benjamin 1973, 259). They have envisioned a just society which will be 'collective, terrestrial, imminent, and total' though not 'miraculous', but rather the product of a history of struggle.

In this article I argue for the continuing importance and pleasure of the utopian tradition in feminist theory and politics. I suggest that the struggle to imagine the desired or beloved community has been and must be conducted in the literary – though not only there. The 'literary' here I take to extend from works of fiction and academic criticism through popularising polemic to the journalism of the dailies and the weekly women's magazines.

To pursue the vision of the future, I look back from the 1990s to the 1890s, another moment in which sexual politics became entangled with narratives of endings. The argument that there is much in common between the 'myths, metaphors and images of sexual crises and apocalypse' which mark that 'fin de siecle' and our own is not original (Showalter 1991, 3). At this millennial moment, the 1890s have been defined by feminist, gay and queer theorists as a time when the boundaries of sex and gender difference began to be challenged and to shift

(Dollimore 1991, esp. 1–35; Sedgwick, 1991 esp. 91; Showalter 1991; Sinfield 1994).

In that decade, too, sexual politics became inseparable from the politics of representation, not only in 'new' novels but in the letters pages of popular papers, in the satiric verse of *Punch* and in articles in middle class journals. The meaning of the 'New Journalism', like the 'New Woman', was contested, hailed both as the promise of a radically better order and as the evidence of a decadent culture. It is to this relationship between the category confusions of the new sexuality and the heterogeneous literature of the new press that we can most usefully look from the 1990s.

I therefore revisit that historical comparison in the spirit of Walter Benjamin's thesis, which was itself informed by the judaic apocalyptic tradition. I seek not to articulate the past 'as it really was' but to 'seize hold of memory as it flashes up at a moment of danger' (Benjamin, 1973, 257). In the 'time of the now' which for us is the late twentieth century, the memory of the 1890s flashes up as a crucial moment for our understanding both of what it means to be gendered, sexed and embodied selves and of how such meanings get made in and through the literary.

II. *The New Decadence*

Fin de siècle, (1890), a phrase used as an adj., characteristic of the end of the (nineteenth) century; advanced; modern; also decadent.
Shorter Oxford Dictionary

'Not to be "new" is, in these days, to be nothing'
H.D. Traill, 1897. 'The New Fiction and Other Essays', London: Hurst and Blackett, p. 1.

The 1890s defined itself in terms of endings though these were characterised by entropy rather than apocalypse. Max Nordau's *Degeneration* was not published in English until 1895, but the idea of a culture marked by individual and collective debility was pervasive even before its appearance (Jackson 1976, esp. 55ff; Stokes 1989, 11). The phrase *fin de siècle* itself, which had been in circulation since the start of the decade, carried powerful connotations of decadence, not least because it was French and therefore immoral. Ideas of degeneration and decadence combined a Social Darwinist concern about Britain's place in the world with anxieties about the nature of the embodied and specifically the sexual self.

The coincidence in 1895 of the publication of *Degeneration* with the public disgrace of Oscar Wilde confirmed an already current symbolic identification of the degenerate, the artist and the homosexual (Jackson 1976, 66). The 'decadent' became both signifier and agent of a cultural crisis in which the nature of masculine sexuality and the place of 'art' in modern culture were caught up. Deciphering the text of masculinity and the male body had always involved the difficulty of defining marital status, which was not central to masculinity as it was to femininity. Now in the mid 1890s male heterosexuality itself was brought into question. Gender, sexuality and bodily difference no longer seemed to be mapped neatly onto each other.

As an artist the decadent also posed questions about the relation of art and life. Degeneration thus became a matter simultaneously of social morality and of the nature of texts, both bodily and written. Wilde's writing and his life made evident the radical instability of representation, the impossibility of reading off the truth, either from the social self or the work of art. Wilde, the married man and leading figure of the literary-fashionable world, creator of *Dorian Grey*, had been discovered to have hidden in his attic the picture of his raddled diseased self. But was that picture the truth or itself a representation? Did Nature imitate Art rather than the other way around, as Wilde had always claimed?

The decadent was thus not only the symbol of the end of the era but a type both of a new kind of self and a new kind of art (Jackson 1976, esp. 17–32). Pater's *Renaissance* was read as promising a new fusion of Art and experience. Wilde's *Soul of Man Under Socialism* brilliantly combined the decadent and utopian. However, the utopian moment of decadence seemed to end with Wilde's disgrace in 1895. Looking back on the decade, Yeats described how the promise of the 1890s poets was dissipated but was uncertain whether it was the lyric form or the material life which made them the 'Tragic Generation' (Yeats 1955, 300). Stokes argues cogently, that it was the popular press which killed both Wilde and the utopian possibilities he embodied (Stokes 1989, 12 and ff).

Certainly, by the end of the century the dominant versions of masculinity were those of the Boer War, of Henty's boys' stories and Kipling's *Stalky and Co*. Its games were played out on the cricket field and the boundaries of Empire rather than in the little magazine. But in the silence at the heart of that masculinity, with its cult of male bonding and its delight in male physical prowess, the love that dares not speak its name continued to resonate (Bristow 1991; Sedgwick 1991).

In the first half of the decade, however, the imagery of decadence was intertwined with the language of beginnings. Apparently quite unconnected cultural and political movements were identified – or identified themselves – as radically new. 'The New Journalism' heralded the era of the modern mass media. The New Critics discussed the visual arts and reviewers dissected The New Fiction, specifically New Woman Fiction and its relationship to the New Sexuality and the New Hedonism. The re-emergence of working class and radical politics was evident in the New Unions, in new socialist parties (the S.D.F. and the I.L.P.) and in attempts at new kinds of community like the Fellowship of the New Life. According to Edward Carpenter, sexual love 'Came of Age'; certainly sexology appeared as a new if not a fully mature discipline (Carpenter 1896).

It was in this context that The New Woman, also singular and capitalised, was named, in implicit distinction from an 'Old' or more often a 'True' femininity (Ardis 1990, 10–11; Jordan 1983). The New Woman embodied a utopian hope for the remaking of gender but was at the same time linked with the degenerate as equally unhealthy, equally 'morbid' in her refusal of the God-given distinction of sexual difference. This was not surprising since 'Newness' was both differentiated from and synonymous with decadence.

The label 'New' was only one of several attached to those women who criticised traditional femininity. Sometimes they were 'Advanced' or 'Modern'. Gissing named them 'Odd' (Gissing 1893). In 1894, a series of articles in the *Nineteenth Century* on 'The Revolt of the Daughters' gave rise to the hostile tag, 'Revolting Daughters' (NC XXXV 1894, 23ff; 424ff). Eliza Lynn Linton, their most vociferous critic, had denounced them as 'Wild Women' and 'Shrieking Sisters' (NC XXX 1891, 79ff; 455ff). Linton had also been responsible for one of the most persistent coinages of the 1860s, the 'Girl of the Period', which like such mid-century terms as 'Redundant' and 'Strong-minded' shadowed the meaning of The New Woman. Each of these names was contested; each indicated a different line of fracture in the structure of True Femininity.

This frenzy of name-calling was a symptom of cultural anxiety and an assertion of the power to control through naming (Ardis 1990, 11). Eliza Lynn Linton, Walter Besant and other critics of the New Woman named her always as the opposite of 'True Woman', a femininity which they explicitly identified with the white English middle class. Linton in particular took the early Victorian ideal of the English middle class domestic woman and reworked it in the context of late Victorian imperialism. Using a Social Darwinist rhetoric of racial competition, she claimed true femininity was embodied in English women:

> A breath of the strong Norse life still lingers about them and makes them emphatically the fit companions and worthy mothers of men. . . . They move on grander, more heroic lines [than French, Italian or German women] and the ideal English woman stands among those white-armed daughters of the gods who know how to command respect while giving love. (*Woman*, 3 Jan. 1890, 1)

The rhetorical energy deployed to define True Woman, like the plethora of names for her opposite, made the meaning of both ever more radically unstable. The campaign for female suffrage which had its roots in the 1860s was sustained throughout the 1890s and burst into life again in 1903 when the Pankhursts founded the WSPU. But in the 1890s political representation was only one aspect of public controversy about the power to represent women culturally. Of course this struggle was not 'new' but in the 1890s it took on a particular intensity and, as with the concept of decadence, a moment seemed to open up when a radical shift in the meaning of gendered identity seemed possible.

III. *The Politics of Representation: The New Journalism*

The crucial site for that struggle was the press, which was going through its own crisis of 'the New' in the 1890s. Although its meaning, too, was disputed, the New Journalism can be characterised textually by the use of the 'tit-bit', the breaking up of the page with headlines and illustration, and by the move towards a more conversational tone and 'the personal note', especially in that New Journalistic genre, the interview. Organisationally and economically, it was marked by the emergence and rise to dominance of the great press barons, Harmsworth, Newnes, and Pearson. Their empires were built on extensive advertising, flotation on the stock exchange and the exploitation of the most-up-to-date technology.

Like the New Woman, the New Journalism was a concept shaped by cultural anxiety. Matthew Arnold, who was credited with inventing the phrase, linked the New Journalism specifically with the new voters, the 'democracy' who 'have many merits but among them is not that of

being in general, reasonable people who think fairly and seriously'
(Arnold 1887, 638). Even sympathetic critics feared that the

> determination to arrest, amuse or startle which has transformed our
> Press during the last fifteen years [meant] the mass of readers . . .
> [were] all alike being carefully trained to a distaste for intellectual
> exertion, a dread of being bored, a need for mental relaxation and a
> coarse habitual tickling of the senses.
>
> (March-Phillipps 1895, 181, 187)

The class anxieties in this were explicit but gender politics also
entered into and shaped the new press and its coarse pleasures – as the
press crucially shaped the meaning of gender. For Harmsworth, the
future Lord Northcliffe, it was the woman reader rather than the new
voter who was 'at the heart' of the New Journalism (Clarke 1950, 84;
Pound 1959, 200, 202). Newnes, the first of the new press barons,
conceived that archetypal new magazine *Tit-Bits* as he read his wife
'titbits' from the newspaper over the tea table (Friederichs 1911, 55).
Identifying the woman at home as the reader of the new journalism
made 'the ladies' page an almost inevitable feature' even of daily papers
(with the exception of the *Times*) (March-Phillips 1895, 186).

It also made the magazine for women central to the business strategy
of the new press houses and so of the whole industry. Harmsworth set
up a subsidiary company to produce cheap but 'wholesome' domestic
magazines for women. In the mid-1890s Pearson and Newnes joined in
with their penny journals; middle price and middle class magazines with
titles like *Woman at Home* and *Hearth and Home* were launched, and a
number of up-market weeklies, including *The Lady's Illustrated* and *The
Gentlewoman*, appeared as rivals to the long-running *Queen*. The
'woman's magazine' emerged into that important place in popular
publishing which it has retained for a century.

New Journalism thus opened up spaces both material and discursive
for New Women to occupy. The establishment in 1895 of the Institute
of Women Journalists confirmed what was evident from any magazine
or journal, that women now had access to print where they could earn
their living and engage in contemporary debates. The handful of lively
but short-lived radical journals for women which appeared in the 1890s
was followed by the rich flowering of the early twentieth-century
feminist press (Doughan and Sanchez 1987). In the women's magazine
femininity was central. It was simultaneously assumed as the given of
its readers and as an always unfinished project, a process in which the
magazine provided guidance for its readers. This created a space in

which the nature of gendered identity could be addressed or even played with as Oscar Wilde did in his short period as editor of *Woman's World* in the late 1880s (Brake 1994).

Yet within these potentially utopian spaces men and women were still differently positioned. It may be, as Walter Besant, founder of the Society of Authors, argued, that the title 'Man of Letters' now included many women, but this formulation itself encoded the masculinity of the professional writer (Besant 1899, 1). The enormous expansion in periodical reading aimed at women did not necessarily give women power even in the editorial offices of these magazines. Most of the editors of women's magazines were men, even in some cases of papers which purported to be edited by women (March-Phillipps 1894, 665). *Woman*, for example, a penny magazine launched in 1890 with a claim to be 'advanced', was throughout the 1890s edited by men, firstly by Fitzroy Gardiner and then by Arnold Bennett. Yet they consistently used female pseudonyms and concealed their masculine editorial identity, an indication at once of the new power of femininity in the popular press and its limitations.

Those limitations were evident in that none of the purely commercial women's magazines from the penny domestic weeklies through the middle class monthlies to the 'class papers' like *The Queen* identified the New Woman as their reader. She was a rich source of copy, subject of jokes, competitions, stories and interviews but her function was to demarcate the boundaries of True Womanhood. New Woman was thus constantly produced for readers as an undesirable but nevertheless as an alternative femininity. This process in itself kept open the utopian possibilities of what may be called an 'opppositional consciousness'. Since no text can absolutely control how it is read, women readers were sometimes able to appropriate, or in Foucauldian terms to reverse, the discourse of 'new womanhood' and to claim it for themselves.

The difficulty of containing the disruptive presence of the New Woman was acute even in the expensive ladies' weeklies which concentrated on fashion and Society. Claiming to be 'newspapers' for women, *The Queen* and its rivals regularly reported on campaigns for women's access to higher education, middle class jobs and political power at national and local level (e.g. *Queen* XLVI (1869), 46, 47, 50, 141–2; LXXVIII (1885) 412; LXXXIX (1891) 274 etc.). *The Gentlewoman* assumed that 'gentlewomen' could never be 'New', yet when it ran a poll on female suffrage among a readership it claimed as 47,000, out of the 9,459 who voted 8,301 voted 'yes' to votes for women. Such

a response drew on the utopian potential of the New Woman to read
the magazine against the grain.[2]

IV. *The New Woman and the New Sexuality*

In 1888 Mona Caird had asked *Daily Telegraph* readers 'Is Marriage a
Failure?'. As the decadent followers of Walter Pater unsettled the
equation of masculinity with a heterosexual maleness, so new women
questioned the absolute correlation of femininity and female sexuality
with marriage and motherhood. Caird's articles provoked 27,000 letters, many of them answering 'yes' and the correspondence continued
to circulate in book form (Stokes 1989, 23). Even determinedly domestic middle class magazines like *Woman at Home* invited correspondence on whether it was possible for women to be 'Happy Though
Married' (*Woman at Home* V (1895–6) 315ff) and the clergyman author
of the popular book *Happy Though Married* wrote on marital problems
in the penny domestic magazine, *Home Chat* (e.g. *Home Chat* 3 Dec.,
1898, 590). The New Woman heroine of Grant Allen's 1895 novel,
The Woman Who Did, was shocking precisely because she refused to
marry her lover.

Significantly, she did not refuse motherhood. Richard le Gallienne
was more liberal than most of his contemporaries when he urged in an
article on 'The New Womanhood', 'Let women become senior wran-
glers, lawyers, doctors, anything they please, as long as they remain
mothers' (Le Gallienne 1894, 1). More often what Penny Boumelha
calls 'socio-biology' was invoked to argue that the 'learned or muscular
woman' was unnatural and that therefore 'the New Woman if a mother
at all' would bring forth monstrous progeny, 'stunted and Hydroce-
phalic children' with unimaginable consequences for the future of the
race (quoted Boumelha 1982, 22).

Like the feminised aesthete or artist, the masculinised New Woman
posed a threat to the foundation of society, the family centred on the
heterosexual couple. However, there were radical differences even here
between men and women. There was no positive public discourse,
however coded, for female same-sex desire surrounding the New
Woman. Woman-woman relationships might be, indeed often were,

---

[2] The debate around the New Woman and New Journalism is taken up in
an extended form in my forthcoming book, *A Magazine of Her Own?: Domesticity and Desire in the Woman's Magazine* (Routledge 1996).

passionate but they could not be defined as erotic (Weeks 1981, 11; Vicinus 1985, 187–210 and passim; see James 1896).

Nevertheless, the New Woman was popularly identified with an apocalyptic break-down of the natural or God-given order which ordained sexual difference. Her characteristic props, the cigarette and the latch-key, were not only themselves phallic symbols but signifiers of a reversal of gender roles. This view entered deeply into the popular imagination. Women readers who entered a competition to define the New Woman in the penny domestic journal *Home Chat* in 1895 castigated her for disfiguring 'God's masterpiece' and showing 'mannishness minus manliness'. One contestant in the comic rhyme characteristic of these debates contrasted the New Woman who

> puts on clothes she didn't ought
> And apes a man in word and thought

with the True Woman who

> . . . throws not sex away,
> Is always lady-like, yet gay. (*Home Chat* 21 Sept. 1895, 29)

However, even in this competition there was evidence that the utopian promise of the idea of the New Woman persisted in the popular imagination. One entry described Her as 'the link between the Old failed woman and the True Woman of the future' and the winning entry from a reader in Bradford, Yorkshire, ran:

> A cage-bird late confined to narrow range
> What marvel if awhile to uses strange
> She puts her new found freedom and essays
> To rival man in foolish antic ways.
> Smile but condemn not, thus her wing she'll try
> For nobler flights she'll use them by and by. (ibid.)

V. *The Politics of Representation: New Women Fiction*

Such competitions were not only between readers for the magazine's prizes but between competing meanings of the New Woman and her significance in *fin-de siècle culture*. In mid-decade this second order contest emerged at the centre of the controversy over the New Woman. The problem of literary representation became bound up with the meaning of 'woman' as a gendered and sexual being. This was made explicit in the critical debates about what were appropriate topics, languages and forms for the novel and above all for the novel read and written by women (Ardis 1990; Boumelha 1982; Cunningham 1978; Flint 1993; Pykett 1992).

Controversies over women's reading of fiction had been endemic throughout the century (Flint 1993). In the 1880s and 1890s they took on a new edge, particularly because new women like Sarah Grand and Mona Caird, as well as men like George Moore, Hardy and Gissing, made women's access to sexual knowledge crucial not only to their particular fictions but to the institutions of fiction publishing and circulation. (Caird 1894; Grand 1888, Hardy 1891; Moore 1885; Griest 1970, 87ff). In the mid-1890s fiction moved into the centre of the struggle over the meaning of 'The New Woman' and her sexuality.

It was not only her critics who argued that 'The True Advanced Woman is not at all that latch-key licensed, tobacco-tainted, gala contaminated Frankenstein which . . . strides up and down the pages of modern literature' (*Idler* IX 1894, 'Advanced Woman Number', 209). However, the claim that the New Woman was *merely* a figment of the literary imagination was, as Ann Ardis argues, mainly deployed as a strategy by those who sought to contain the threat she posed (Ardis 1990, 11). Locating her as 'a literary' as distinct from a 'real' phenomenon also denied the power of fiction as a cultural force and was part of a larger set of negotiations over the nature of cultural representation and the place of the literary in social movements.

In those debates New Woman fiction was only one genre. It cannot be separated from the rest of 'literature' and in particular the New Journalism in which it was serialised, reviewed, and satirised and where its authors were interviewed and photographed. The important genres here were the satiric sketch, the polemical article and the illustrated interview or potted life of a 'Notable Woman', which was a staple of general and women's periodicals in the 1890s. *Punch* had installed the genre of comic rhyme at the centre of the New Woman debate and the much quoted *Punch* rhyme was perhaps the most succinct and witty expression of the contradictory power of these literary representations:

> There is a New Woman and what do you think?
> She lives upon nothing but Foolscap and ink!
> But though Foolscap and Ink are the whole of her diet,
> This nagging New Woman can never be quiet!
> (*Punch* 26 May 1894, 252; quoted Ardis 1990, 11;
> Jordan 1983, 19; Rubinstein 1986, 22)

New Woman was at once a literary phenomenon and constantly exceeded attempts to label her as 'merely' literary. Indeed these attempts themselves kept open the possibility for readers to appropriate the concept and make it the basis for refusing to be quiet in their turn. In that process self-confessed fictions played a crucial though not an exclusive part.

VI. *New Woman and Working Man*

The complex sexual/textual politics of the new femininity was further complicated by its relationship with other contemporary struggles to define and bring about a more just society. Of these the most important were the socialist movements which identified class rather than gender as the key to social transformation.

According to Ellen Jordan, the name New Woman in its singular and capitalised form, was crystalised in 1894 by the novelist Ouida (Jordan 1983). Ouida castigated as 'unmitigated bores' that twosome 'The Working Man' and 'The New Woman' who

> meet us at every page of literature written in the English tongue and each is convinced that on its own special W hangs the future of the world. (quoted Ardis 1990, 11)

In the late 1880s and early 1890s it was around 'the special W' of The Working Man and within the various socialist groups and Labour Churches that the vision of a future just society was most explicitly pursued. Like true millenarians these socialists envisioned that future as collective, terrestrial and to be brought into being through the action of history. Central to their utopian project, therefore, was the 'education of desire' (Thompson 1976, 791). This was enacted through the dynamic relationship between social organisation and literary texts, whether of political analysis and polemic or of fictions, most notably William Morris's *News from Nowhere* which was serialised in *Commonweal* in 1890.

In linking the two 'Ws' Ouida suggested they were competing and mutually exclusive, linked only by being equally boring. Certainly the 'Daughters' whose 'Revolt' so engaged the middle-class press during 1894 had worked within a class-specific model of femininity. They had asked *only* to be treated 'as their brother', that is be allowed to exercise their 'right to individual development' (Smith 446, 449). But their demand for self-development assumed the location of the brother in the upper-middle class. Significantly, this was precisely the criticism made of them in the penny weekly magazine *Woman* by Walter Crane (*Woman* 1894, 24 Jan., 15; 28 Feb., 3, 4).

The problem of whether the New Woman, like the True Woman, made universalising claims for a class-specific femininity returned again and again in the 1890s. In the popular women's press it was caught up in a set of debates around the relative meanings of the words 'woman' and 'lady', each of which had historically tied gender and class together. Ruskin's argument made in the still immensely influential essay, 'Of Queen's Gardens', was that every woman now called herself 'a lady' (Ruskin 1900, 120–1). But Wilde had famously refused to take on the editorship of the *Lady's World* unless it became *Woman's World* since the word lady had acquired the tint of vulgarity (Nowell-Smith 1958, 256).

Another searcher after the 'truth' of femininity, writing in *Woman*, declared 'a plague on all your houses' in a characteristic New Journalistic/ New Woman rhyme:

> What do our sisters say to this?
> Are they such matters prim in?
> And do they mean to urge the plan
> That 'women' cannot 'ladies' be,
> That ladies can't be women?
>
> By all means let them, if they choose,
> This new demand be grim in:
> Let the new Ladies have their will
> If only they will leave us still
> Our good old English women.
>
> ('Truth,' *Woman* 23 Jan. 1895, 8)

Those who refused this retreat to a 'True' femininity continued to wrestle with the problem of how gender oppression related to other kinds of oppression, specifically those of class. They gave no single answer to the question. The radical magazine *Shafts* was launched on the assumption that it could address 'women and the working class' simultaneously and in parallel, a project which proved productive but curiously fractured.

Within the various socialist groups, debate on the place of gender relations in a future just society had been brought into sharp focus by the translation into English of two major theoretical works by German socialists, Bebel's *Woman in the Past, Present and Future*, also translated as *Woman and Socialism* and Engels' *The Origin of the Family, Private Property and the State*. Bebel's work, which was widely read and referred to in British socialist circles, offered the utopian promise of women's future liberation (Hunt, unpub.). The desire for and commitment to a future in which 'kindly and humane relations between the sexes' would replace the 'modern bourgeois property-marriage' maintained by 'universal venal prostitution' was written into the Manifesto of the Socialist League (Thompson 1976, 735). Stephen Yeo argues that the attempts to create 'A New Life' through the religion of socialism were doomed from the mid-1890s, not least by the emergence of the Independent Labour Party with its concern for the creation of an electorally oriented party-machine (Yeo 1976). But its utopian vision profoundly shaped not only the future of socialism but the thinking of New Women like Eleanor Marx and Olive Schreiner.

VII. A *Utopian Text*: Dreams

It was her refusal to respect the boundaries of traditional categories whether sexual or textual which characterised the New Woman and made her both threat and promise. Though Olive Schreiner's *Story of an African Farm* (hereafter *African Farm*) had been published in 1883, it offered both the prototype of the transgressive new woman in its protagonist, Lyndall, and enacted a formal refusal of nineteenth-century literary conventions.

Its author herself refused to conform to the categories of late nineteenth-century culture. Brought up in southern Africa, she was never at home in the London world to which she came in 1881 with her novel in her luggage. Hailed by decadent critics like Symonds and Wilde, who published one of her allegories in *Woman's World*, she was determined to be read by the working class (First 1980, 186). For her the problem of the new sexuality was a theoretical one which she debated with Carpenter and Havelock Ellis of the Society of the New Life as well as in the Men's and Women's Club (Rowbotham 1977, 42–3 and passim; Walkowitz 1992, 135ff). But it was also the agonising personal difficulty of negotiating desire and social convention as a single woman (First 1980, 124–182 and passim).

Schreiner's writing likewise refused the categorisations of literary genre and particularly those which separate the 'novel' from 'theoretical work' or polemic. Her reputation was established with *African Farm* but the work for which she became best known was *Women and Labour*, the theoretical, polemical, mystical book which became the 'Bible of the Women's Movement' in the early twentieth century. As with her *oeuvre*, so each of her works individually transgressed the norms of literary convention. *African Farm* broke with the demands of nineteenth-century realism. The text was disrupted by polemic and the allegorical story of the Hunter and the Bird of Truth.

Here, too, Schreiner opened up possibilities for the writers of the 1890s. Though women were beginning to question the social institution of marriage, the power of the socio-literary convention, which made marriage the only positive fictional resolution for the female protagonist, persisted (Duplessis 1985, 1–3). In novels by men, even those who claimed to be sympathetic like Hardy and Allen, there was no utopian end imaginable for the New Woman. She had to die (Allen 1895: Hardy 1895). In some fictions by New Women, however, the utopian broke through – either in whole texts or in disruptive moments, visions and polemic, as in the the Tenor and the Boy episode in Sarah Grand's *The Heavenly Twins* (1893) and most notably in Schreiner's own *Dreams*. Such utopian elements disrupted both the fictional convention of narrative closure and the social convention which equated 'the beloved community' exclusively with the recreation of the family unit, the heterosexual couple and their offspring.

In *Dreams*, published in 1890, the year after she returned to Africa, Schreiner brought together short allegorical pieces written over a number of years. It was the most thoroughly utopian of her books, as she signalled by its dedication to 'A Small Girl-Child, who may live to grasp somewhat of that which for us is yet sight, not touch'. Schreiner claimed that these pieces embodied 'all her socialistic strivings' (First 1980, 185). Yet they also addressed the place and nature of sexuality and love. She sought, therefore, to reconfigure desire in terms both of the social and the erotic, recasting in a utopian mold those questions she wrestled with as a new woman; the nature of oppression and exploitation, the consequences of forcing women to choose between Love and Freedom, and the historical necessity – as she saw it – for the present generation of women to work for the future society they might never touch.

She made no attempt at direct social comment or at realistic characterisation. The writing is abstract and elevated; the characters are Man, Woman, God, the Dreamer, the Hunter after Truth; the settings are equally allegorical – the Ruined Chapel, the sleeper's bed, 'the almighty mountains of Dry-facts and Realities'. In 'Three Dreams in a Desert' Schreiner evoked the Africa of her childhood memories, but it was as a dream landscape in which 'woman' lies in the sands of history, struggling to rise.

Schreiner appropriated for the late nineteenth century the genres of allegory and dream which had been re-worked in the English literary tradition from *Pearl* through Langland's *Piers Ploughman*, to Bunyan's *Pilgrim's Progress* and beyond. She combined this with the tradition of utopianism which her contemporaries Bellamy and Charlotte Perkins Gilman as well as Morris in their different ways also revitalised. Like them, Schreiner had to wrestle with how to image, indeed how to imagine, the just society. She deployed but also subverted those two most potent symbols of the utopian tradition, the Garden of Eden and the family based on the married couple.

At the end of *Women and Labour*, Schreiner returned to the 'dream of a garden' and in *Dreams* the natural cycle of renewal and growth is evoked directly in stories like 'In a Ruined Chapel'. Set in an idealised Italian landscape, this ends with the 'blue, blue skies', olive trees and rain on dry ground (*Dreams* 1893, 111–12). 'Three Dreams' also ends with an image of natural renewal: 'Then the sun passed down behind the hills; but I knew that next day he would rise again' (op. cit., 85). Such images are rarely used simply, however. The front cover of the first British edition showed a rising sun poised over a sun-dial, for the sun also represented time and human history which would deliver the promised future.

More often Schreiner's allegories work with and through images of the social including the couple and the family. In 'Three Dreams in a Desert' the traditional couples of 'brave women' and 'brave men' walk on the hills of the future Heaven but beside them 'the women also held each other's hands' (op. cit., 84). In 'I Thought I Stood' the concepts of Brother and Sisterhood recall socialist usage but here take on both class and gender meanings. The Woman who arraigns her Brother Man before the throne of God is forced to acknowledge that her own feet are red with the blood of her Sisters on whom she has trodden. Only when she has lain beside her Sister in the street can she return to God, seeking not vengeance against Man but his redemption (op. cit., 125–9).

In 'The Sunlight Lay Across My Bed', the most extended of her allegories, Schreiner imaged a series of hells and heavens, starting with the 'Hell' of a culture in which bodies are broken like grapes in the wine-press to provide the banquet for the few. In the highest Heaven of this story there are no divisions and no differences, so there is no coupling or family. Its symbolic inhabitant is androgynous, for though sex reigns supreme in the lowest heaven, 'in the higher it is not noticed and in the highest it does not exist' (op. cit., 175). 'I cannot forgive – I love', the epigraph to 'In a Ruined Chapel' embodied Schreiner's utopian ideal. Forgiveness still implied unequal power relations. The only answer to division was the renewing power of love, but love was neither simply social nor sexual.

These parables of regeneration and reconciliation which Schreiner set against the problems of division and exploitation appealed across the spectrum of contemporary readerships and into the next generation. Even though *Dreams* was produced at first in a relatively expensive form and was, Schreiner argued, addressed to the middle class, it was taken up and read by working class women who had found *African Farm* spoke to and for them (First 1980, 185). Co-operative Guild activists writing in the 1920s recorded it among the books which influenced them (Davies 1977, 129). According to Schreiner's biographers, the suffragettes in Holloway prison read *Dreams* not only as an inspiration and comfort but 'like an ABC railway guide to our journey' (quoted First 1980, 185).

VIII.   The 1990s: The impossibility of Utopia?

In the 1990s we lack maps for our journey or dreams of a possible future to resist the apocalyptic scenarios of an Aids epidemic, destruction of the planet, endemic warfare or more mundanely the fragmentation and division of society, racism, job insecurity, lack of decent housing, the terror of unloved old age and incapacity.

In Britain the Government's attempts to find a way of celebrating the millennium are farcical rather than tragic. The Millennium Commission even bungled the appointment of a chief executive, that most important task of any body in late twentieth-century Britain (*Independent* 1 Jan, 1995, 8–12). Its difficulties are compounded by a contradiction in its very existence, which the Government dimly recognises, namely that the millenarian tradition has never been about top-down management; it has never been consistent with the one Scriptural injunction enacted in current politics from the academic to the xenophobic, namely 'To him that hath shall be given and from him that hath not shall be taken away even what he hath'. The millennium by contrast has always been claimed by the have-nots. Its script is written in a very different poetic. In the biblical tradition of female prophecy exemplified by the word given to Mary by the Gospel writer,

Luke, it has been about feeding the hungry and sending the rich empty away (Luke 1, 53).

The struggle to wrest history from the powerful for the dispossessed, according to Benjamin, can be conducted in the present only by those who *can* turn towards the future (Benjamin 1973, 257). In this last section, I turn from the memory flashed up from the 1890s to consider what visions of the future are available for us in the tradition of feminist utopian thinking. Those inherited symbols of regeneration, the Garden, the married couple and the Family, with their models of hierarchised unity, present particular difficulties for contemporary feminists. Yet across a variety of genres, they have been taken up and reworked, ironically and positively.

In *Nights at the Circus* Carter re-invented the moment when the 1890s became the twentieth century, re-writing not only the historical script but a series of myths which form the cultural legacy of the late twentieth century and its feminisms: the panopticon as symbol of the disciplinary society, Russia as home to both political revolution and mysticism, the brothel as the site of female powerlessness – Carter reworked them all in turn.

Of these inherited tropes Carter took three specifically utopian narratives and reworked them in her fiction. The first is the narrative of running away to the circus. The most famous literary version of the circus as an image of the desired organic community, outside and therefore beyond the injustices of industrial capitalism, was Dickens' *Hard Times*. In our hard times this image has been reworked ironically in a range of media. The circus performer, the aerialiste, is the symbol of desire in Wim Wender's bitter-sweet 'Wings of Desire' while the press retells as farce the story of the Prime Minister who ran away from the circus to be a politician.

Carter rewrote the circus lovingly but also ironically. The love which flowers there is the love of woman for woman; the clown is a philosopher king who goes mad in an alcoholic frenzy; the circus offers pleasure as a source not of escape but of profit. Crucially in this circus the categories which structure our culture are breached. The distinction between human and animal dissolves; Walser becomes a human chicken; the tigers enjoy *lieder*, the mystic pig gives financial advice to the Colonel and the intelligent apes take control of their act, not to liberate themselves but to negotiate a better contract. Formally, too, Carter mixes the categories of realism and fantasy. Fevvers escapes a fate worse than death by leaping onto a toy train out of a Fabergé egg.

Secondly, in Fevvers, Carter combines the image of the aerialist as object of desire with the winged woman as symbol of liberation. Fevvers is the 1890s New Woman, re-written with the same ironic affection as is the circus. Literal embodiment of the fantasies of liberation and of the Winged Victory, Fevvers is both late nineteenth-century music hall artist and mythical figure. She is a paradox for, as Walser tells himself, if her wings are 'real' then she is a 'marvellous monster', a freak; but if she is a woman (and she owes it to herself to remain a woman) then she is indeed 'a wonder' (Carter 1984, 161). Carter sustains the paradox throughout, never allowing the reader to know which to believe.

Finally and most boldly, Carter re-writes the cliché of the romance narrative and its simultaneous conclusion/ consummation with the heroine at last in the arms of the man who has desired her and whom she desires. This hack narrative is reproduced as the story of the hack journalist, the anti-hero, Walser. Carter thus symbolically links the New Journalism and the New Woman. Walser's identity is not so much a paradox as constantly in flux. Throughout the novel, he rewrites himself, becoming in turn journalist, clown, shaman and finally, lover. Up to the moment when 'the moveable feast of midnight' precipitates the lovers in 'ignorance and bliss' into a new – that is the twentieth – century, Walser cannot stop taking himself apart and re-inventing himself again (Carter 1984, 294).

At the moment of truth, the moment of consummation, when the virginity of the bride is traditionally brought to proof, the whole story dissolves into a joke – but whether the joke is on Walser, the fooled husband, or on the fooled reader remains ambivalent. Just as Fevvers tells him not to believe everything he writes in the papers, so we are invited as readers not to ask for proof but to enjoy the game of 'writing up' the story (op. cit., 294). Carter rewrites the romance, not to maintain the natural and social necessity of the heterosexual couple but to assert that history is 'a giant comedy' rather than the tragedy of the apocalyptic imagination (op. cit., 295).

Like Schreiner's work of the 1880s, Carter's writing of the 1980s prefigures that of the 90s. Just as playfully but in a different genre and a different voice, Donna Haraway's 'A Cyborg Manifesto' offers an analogous utopianism. Fevvers, Carter's winged woman, like Haraway's cyborg is the product of myth and history, or rather of mythic history. Haraway's project of re-inventing nature parallels Carter's re-invention of history. Both distrust 'the natural' as a utopian refuge. Carter, like her characters, was 'basically out of sympathy with landscape [and got] the shivers on Hampstead bloody Heath' (Carter 1984, 197; Ward Jouve 1994).

In her 'A Cyborg Manifesto', Haraway argues that in the 1990s we must abandon stories of the return to Edenic wholeness which depend on the myth of original unity represented by the phallic mother. Such myths have always been ambivalent for women who represent both the Mother and Nature. Moreover they construct the present in terms of deepening divisions, especially between the natural and the techno-logical or man-made, and offer a hierarchised utopia where the tech-nological is contolled in the interests of 'the natural'. Haraway rejects both this analysis and its solutions. She argues for a creative transgres-sion of the old oppositions which demarcated culture and nature, human and animal, human and machine, public and private, mind and body, and even man and woman. Such category distinctions no longer work. As in Carter's circus, 'man's' absolute superiority over the animal on the basis of intelligence begins to dissolve. So, too, does the absolute distinction between 'man' and machine when the heart pace-maker and the contact lens, even the motor car and computer may be integral to the selves we are.

In our time, according to Haraway, the dream of regeneration on the model of the natural, whether the garden or the 'organic family', is not only irrelevant; it is destructive. Crucially, also, it refuses the positive knowledge which white western feminists have been forced – some-times painfully – to learn, that 'we' cannot legislate for the categories of identity and difference. 'We' are all caught up in a global economy of fragmentation and dispersal. No longer able to name the simple categories to which we belong, we cannot ground the 'potent political myth called "us" ' (Harraway 1991, 155).

As answer to this crisis, Haraway offers not the traditional utopia but the cyborg, a creature from science fiction and robotics whose identity has never been 'natural' or given. Instead of regeneration and the return to an imagined organic community, the cyborg offers replication – the possibility that division and splitting can be creative of radically new forms. These new forms will come about not on the basis of given identities – be they those of gender, 'race' or ability – but through the creation of cyborg societies, affiliation groups dedicated to resisting the apocalyptic fantasies of the politicians and the military. Haraway's vision is of a group committed to holding together in one heterogeneous alliance 'witches, engineers, elders, perverts, Christians, mothers and Leninists' (op. cit., 155). Such a cyborg politics, I would argue, has begun to be manifest in mid-1990s Britain in groups who have come together to resist the Criminal Justice Act, the construction of a new motorway or the deportation of residents on the grounds of their 'race' and in such groups as Women Against Fundamentalism.

In *Nights at the Circus*, Carter looked back to the end of the 1890s and wrote her mythic history around the relationship of sexual politics, the imaginary good community, and writing (whether in the novel or 'in the papers'). Her playful exploration, like Haraway's ironic 'Manifesto', differs absolutely from the popular polemic of 'post-feminists', Naomi Wolf and Katie Roiphe, though they in their different ways also address the future of 'woman'. There are certain common positions. Like Carter and Haraway, both Wolf and Roiphe reject a politics built on the victim status of the category 'woman'. They recognise that the struggle to name 'woman' and to find positive narratives for the future involve rewriting the past across the range of the literary. Wolf argues for example that the woman's magazine should be colonised as a positive space for women to define themselves (Wolf 1991, 58–85).

However, neither Wolf nor Roiphe problematise the category 'woman' or acknowledge the process by which feminists have learned to ask who is the 'we' of feminism and how is it to be created. As bell hooks points out, both Wolf and Roiphe have sought in different ways to appropriate the narrative of feminism for the experience of privileged young white women, denying race and class difference (hooks 1994, 91ff and 101ff).

Against such totalising narratives, bell hooks offers another kind of writing and another kind of vision in the third of my late twentieth-century texts. Her *Outlaw Culture; Resisting Representations* takes up the battle over cultural representation from the position of a black American woman who is now an academic and writer. Mixing autobiography, dialogue, polemic and close reading of specific texts, hooks ends the collection with two utopian pieces, 'Moving into and beyond Feminism; (Just for the Joy of It)' and 'Love as the Practice of Freedom'.

The first of these is a dialogue/interview. For hooks this form enables her to enact as well as explore the complexities of an identity and a cultural politics which resists the univocal. Refusing to confine herself to a 'gender only' or 'race only' subjectivity, she ranges or 'transgresses' across the territory of late twentieth-century popular culture, American politics and her own life experience (hooks 1994, 208). Like Schreiner before her and Haraway her contemporary, hooks wrestles with the problem of how a society without domination can be brought about when differences separate, instead of bond, those 'who really want to change the world' (op. cit., 216). hooks argues for a politics based not on identity, as 'women', but on the 'yearning to be in a more just world'.

For her the 'site of desire and longing might be a potential place for community-building' (op. cit., 217).

The role of art in this politics of desire is crucial. The book consists mainly of critiques of specific examples of popular texts, literary, musical and filmic. hooks' concern is with their representations of 'race', gender and 'the poor', that is with the way power operates in our culture. But her critique is not in the interests of a social realist art but is informed by a belief that the 'function of art is to do more than tell it like it is – it's to imagine what is *possible*'. 'Art' for hooks is inclusive and takes in Madonna's 'Sex' book, Spike Lee's films, rap music, the myth of Columbus.

hooks argues not only that academics must use the tools of critical reading on popular texts but that they must test their theoretical and critical perspectives outside the privileged world of the academy. 'The elaborate shifts in location, thought, and life experience' which cultural critics write about 'as though it were only a matter of individual will' are most difficult for those who lack material means and educational privilege.

> To claim border crossing, the mixing of high and low, cultural hybridity, as the deepest expression of a desired cultural practice in a multicultural democracy means that we must dare to envision ways such freedom of movement can be experienced by everyone.
>
> (op. cit., 5)

Unlike Haraway, hooks is not afraid to use the trope of nostalgia for 'the beloved community' of her past. However, she locates the radical potential of that community not in a myth of the garden but in two specific histories. The first is that of the black neighbourhood where she grew up. This was 'a community' not because it was black but because of 'what we did together' (op. cit., 277). Secondly, she returns to the politics of Martin Luther King and his statement that 'I have decided to love', which for him was the basis both of his politics and of the 'beloved community' (op. cit., 247, 250).

hooks reads a particular history in terms of a utopian future grasped from a present in which she is engaged in the struggle over representations. She thus returns me to Walter Benjamin's 'Theses on the Philosophy of History', which has underpinned the argument of this article. For Benjamin historical transformation would only come about through struggle in the present which was informed by a longing for the future. The shape of that future could not be grasped in images of return, whether to the garden or the Mother. It depended on the work of the historian. History in this thesis does not mean recounting 'the sequence of events like the beads of a rosary'. It is about grasping the past in relation to the danger of the present. The present can then be understood as 'the time of the now', as itself shot through with 'chips of Messianic time' (Benjamin 1973, 265).

Works Cited

Allen, Grant, 1895. *The Woman Who Did*, London: John Lane.

Ardis, Ann, 1990. *New Women, New Novels: Feminism and Early Modernism*, New Brunswick: Rutgers.

Arnold, Matthew, 1887. 'Up to Easter,' *Nineteenth Century* XXI, 629–43.

Benjamin, Walter, 1973 (1940, Eng. tr. 1970). 'Theses on the Philosophy of History,' *Illuminations*, London: Fontana.

Besant, Walter, 1899. *The Pen and the Book*, London: Thomas Burleigh.

Boumelha, Penny, 1982. *Thomas Hardy and Women: Sexual Ideology and Narrative Form*, Brighton: Harvester.

Brake, Laurel, 1994. *Subjugated Knowledges: Journalism, Gender and Literature in the Nineteenth Century*, London: Macmillan.

Bristow, Joseph, 1991. *Empire Boys: Adventures in a Man's World*, London: Harper Collins.

Carpenter, Edward, 1896. *Love's Coming-of-Age*, Manchester: Labour Press.

Caird, Mona, 1894. *The Daughters of Danæus*, London: Bliss, Sands and Foster.

Carter, Angela, 1984. *Nights at the Circus*, London: Chatto and Windus.

Clarke, Thomas, 1950. *Northcliffe in History: an Intimate Study of Press Power*, London: Hutchinson.

Cohn, Norman, 1970 (1957). *The Pursuit of the Millennium*, London: Granada.

Cunningham, Gail, 1978. *The New Woman and the Victorian Novel*, London: Macmillan.

Davies, Margaret Llewelyn (ed.), 1977 (1931). *Life as We Have Known It by Co-Operative Working Women*, London: Virago.

Dollimore, Jonathan, 1991. *Sexual Dissidence: Augustine to Wilde; Freud to Foucault*, Oxford: Oxford U.P.

Duplessis, Rachel Blau, 1985. *Writing Beyond the Ending: Narrative Strategies of Twentieth Century Women Writers*, Bloomington: Indiana U.P.

First, R., and Scott, A., 1980. *Olive Schreiner, A Biography*, London: Deutsch.

Flint, Kate, 1993. *The Woman Reader, 1837–1914*, Oxford: Oxford U.P.

Griest, Guinevere, 1970. *Mudie's Ciruclating Library and the Victorian Novel*, Bloomington: Indiana U.P.

Gissing, George, 1893. *The Odd Women*, London: Lawrence and Bullen.

Grand, Sarah, 1894 (1888). *Ideala: a study from life*, London: Heinemann.

Grosz, Elizabeth, 1992. 'What is feminist theory?', H. Crowley and S. Himmelweit (eds), *Knowing Women: Feminism and Knowledge*, Cambridge: Polity.

Haraway, Donna, 1991. 'A Cyborg Manifesto,' *Simians,Cyborgs and Women; the Re-invention of Nature*, London: Free Association Books.

Hardy, Thomas, 1891. *Tess of the D'urbervilles*, London: Osgood, McIlvaine & Co.

————, 1896 [1895]. *Jude the Obscure*, London: Osgood, McIlvaine & Co.

hooks, bell, 1994. *Outlaw Culture, Resisting Representations*, New York: Routledge.

Hunt, Karen, forthcoming. *Equivocal Feminists, the S.D.F. and the Woman Question*, Cambridge: Cambridge U.P.

Jackson, Holbrook, 1976 (1913). *The Eighteen Nineties*, Brighton: Harvester.

James, Henry, 1886. *The Bostonians*, London: Macmillan.

Jeffreys, Sheila, 1985. *The Spinster and her Enemies: Feminism and Sexuality, 1880–1930*, London: Pandora.

Jordan, Ellen, 1983. 'The Christening of the New Woman, May 1894,' *Victorian Newsletter* XLVIII, 19.

Kermode, F., 1966. *The Sense of an Ending: Studies in the Theory of Fiction*, Oxford: Oxford U.P.

Kushner, Tony, 1992. *Angels in America: a gay fantasia on national themes*. Pt. I: *Millennium Approaches*, London: Nick Hern.

Le Gallienne, Richard, 1894. 'The New Womanhood,' *Woman, Lit. Sup.*, 1.

March-Phillipps, Evelyn, 1894. 'Women's Newspapers,' *Fortnightly Review*, N.S. XLVI, 661–9.

————, 1895. 'The New Journalism,' *The New Review* XII, 182–9.

Moore, George, 1885. *Literature at Nurse, or Circulating Morals*, London: Vizetelly.

Nowell-Smith, Simon, 1985. *The House of Cassell, 1848–1958*, London: Cassell.

O'Connor, T.P., 1889. 'The New Journalism,' *The New Review* I, 423–34.

Pound, R., and Harmsworth, G., 1959. *Northcliffe*, London: Cassell.

Pykett, Lyn, 1992. *The Improper Feminine*, London: Routledge.

Roiphe, Katie, 1994. *Morning After: Sex, Fear and Feminism*, London: Hamish Hamilton.

Rowbotham, S., and Weeks, J., 1977. *Socialism and the New Life: The Personal and Sexual Politics of Edward Carpenter and Havelock Ellis*, London: Pluto.

Rubinstein, David, 1986. *Before the Suffragettes*, Brighton: Harvester.

Ruskin, John, 1900 (1865). 'Of Queen's Gardens,' *Sesame and Lilies*, Portland, Maine: Thomas Mosher.

Sedgwick, Eve Kosofsky, 1991. *The Epistemology of the Closet*, Brighton: Harvester.

Schreiner, Olive, 1893 (1890). *Dreams*, Boston: Roberts Brothers.

Sinfield, Allen, 1994. *The Wilde Century*, London and New York: Cassell.

Showalter, Elaine, 1990. *Sexual Anarchy: Gender and Culture at the Fin de Siècle*, London: Bloomsbury.

Smith, Alys Pearsall, 1894. 'A Reply from the Daughters, II,' *Nineteenth Century* XXXV, 443–50.

Stanley, Liz, 1983. 'Olive Schreiner, New Women, Free Women, All Women,' D. Spender (ed.), *Feminist Theorists*, London: Women's Press.

Stokes, John, 1989. *In the Nineties*, Brighton: Harvester.

Thompson, E.P., 1977. *William Morris: Romantic to Revolutionary*, London: Merlin.

Vicinus, Martha, 1985. *Independent Women: Work and Community for Single Women, 1850–1920*, London: Virago.

Walkowitz, Judith, 1994. *City of Dreadful Delight: Narratives of Sexual Danger in Late-Victorian London*, London: Virago.

Ward Jouve, Nicole, 1994. 'Mother is a Figure of Speech,' L. Sage, (ed.), *Flesh and Mirror: Essays on the Art of Angela Carter*, London: Virago.

Wolf, Naomi, 1990. *The Beauty Myth*, London: Vintage.

Yeats, W.B. 1973 (1950). *Autobiographies*, London: Macmillan.

Yeo, Stephen, 1977. 'A New Life: the Religion of Socialism in Britain, 1883–1896', *History Workshop Journal* IV, 5–56.

Hell innit:
the millennium in Alasdair Gray's Lanark, Martin Amis's London Fields, and Shena Mackay's Dunedin.

PENNY SMITH

WHILE IT CAN BE ARGUED that mere *fin de siecle* inevitably courts disillusionment, the recognition that there is to be no brave new world just around the corner, it is useful to keep in mind that 'for most of human history the idea of the millennium itself has been essentially hopeful' (O'Toole, 29). After Apocalypse comes judgement, and there-after the thousand-year rule by Christ and a panoply of saints. As we approach the third millennium, however, any belief in resurrection has increasingly become the province of suicidal cults: for the rest of us the dancing on the Berlin Wall is over and we watch in growing alarm as the spectres of civil war, genocide, and nuclear vandalism slouch across the landscape of a disintegrating Europe. According to the historian Eric Hobsbawm:

> the European 20th century has already ended with the collapse of the last great utopia of communism and the return of the map of Europe to a shape similar to that before the first world war.
>
> (cited O'Toole, 29)

If, then, the millennium has already encroached into the European consciousness by a couple of decades might it not be that the state of mind that we have come to describe as postmodern is actually better understood as being 'postmillennial'? (A possibility that postmod-ernism, with its underlying sense of ending and crisis, has long been hinting at anyway.) And might it not also be possible that the end of the twentieth century can be pushed back even further than Hobsbawm suggests? As far, say, as the mid twentieth century? For in the three texts to be discussed here, *Lanark* (1981), *London Fields* (1989), and *Dunedin* (1992), there is a sense that as we approach the year 2000 we find ourselves looking not forward but back, to the catastrophe that has cast its shadow across the second half of the twentieth century, the Second World War.

I

If the period since the war has witnessed the occasional preemptive obituary of history, the death of the novel has been hailed with even greater regularity. What call for the novel when narrative has leapt from the printed page to the computer screen? In the last decade of the twentieth century the once-upon-a-time reader is transformed into either a hero/player, negotiating/narrating a path through levels of increasing difficulty, or a writer/programmer disappearing into the variable choice that is the hypertext, where it is guaranteed that no readings can ever possibly be the same. Whereas narrative as was, on the page, on the stage, on the cinema and television screen, did (despite readings translated through gender, race, class, age, sexuality) have a certain, albeit fragile, stability, we are now faced with the possibility of endless instability, of no shared readings being possible, or desirable.

Postmodernism supposes the predominance of the electronic media, but it is also apparent that narrative is demonstrating a determination to survive in a resurgence of oral tradition and in the novel's own ability to incorporate, and even to thrive on, instability. Readers can no longer be entirely sure of just where they are, or when the next leap – in genre, difficulty, *faith* – will be necessary. Alasdair Gray's *Lanark* – 'possibly the first Scottish metafiction' (Imhoff, 75) – is a prime example of this.

The fragmented text that is *Lanark* reflects, however, not only contemporary pressures on narrative but, more specifically, the fragmented consciousness of the protagonist(s), Thaw/Lanark, and the state of late capitalist society. We begin with what appears to be a realist text, as a man of about twenty-four sits on the balcony of a bohemian cafe in what might be any decade, in any city, of the twentieth century. Realism, however, quickly lurches into science fantasy: the man sits staring out into the darkness not in hope of enlightenment, but in the hope of catching a glimpse of sunlight. The city he finds himself in is Unthank (a fact not discovered till the next stage of his journey, this piece of information being kept secret by the civic authorities for 'security reasons', 31). Unthank is a thankless place, where it is always dark, it is impossible to keep track of time's passing, and people are afflicted with attacks of 'dragonhide' (from which Lanark suffers), 'twittering rigor', 'softs' or 'mouths'. Comparing his symptoms with those of Gay, a woman patron of the cafe, Lanark is appalled when she unclenches her palm to reveal a mouth, through which Sludden, the leader of one of the cafe's cliques speaks to him. Gay is Sludden's mouthpiece, in every sense, and Lanark suddenly realizes where he is: '. . . this is hell!' (45).

Up till now he hasn't been sure. He's arrived in the city on a train, nameless and with no memory (something he's made sure of by throwing away the papers and diary he discovers in his knapsack). All he is sure of is that he craves sunlight, that he couldn't be an artist – when Sludden suggests this occupation he says he has nothing to tell people (6) – and that he has arrived in a place where people randomly disappear when the lights (the electric variety) go out. Some individuals refuse to disappear quietly: her last lodger, Lanark's landlady informs him, 'left a hell of a mess . . . And his screams!' (13). But when Lanark's turn comes he goes voluntarily. A giant mouth (or vagina) opens in the ground at his feet announcing 'I am the way out' (47), and Lanark leaps in. Only to find himself reborn in an even stranger place, the institute.

For the reader the institute links the worlds of *Lanark* with our own: Lanark is tended by a doctor who informs him that this is an establishment which has 'been isolated since the outbreak of the second world war' (53), and his supply of reading material includes *Our Wullie's Annual for 1938* and *No Orchids for Miss Blandish*. What we have, then, is a parallel universe, a fracturing of the world as we know it that occurred during the war. This connection with our own here and now is subsequently made clear in the story Lanark hears from the oracle in the Prologue and Books One and Two (the novel begins with Book Three). The connecting passage between the parallel worlds is death: Lanark, Duncan Thaw in his previous life, commits suicide and so finds himself as the nameless man on the train, shunting into an alternative existence.

Or does he? Douglas Gifford argues that the only consistent way to read Gray's novel is as hallucination resulting from mental breakdown (Gifford, 111). But while such a reading is certainly consistent with the realist characterization of Duncan Thaw, the text as a whole strains against such consistency. *Lanark*, with its disrupted chronology and structure, self-reflective notes, allegorically-laden illustrations (see Lee), extravagant layout and typography, not only demands but also deserves an exuberant suspension of disbelief. Duncan Thaw *is* reborn as Lanark. Lanark *does* find himself in the institute, where he falls in love with Rima, with whom he travels through time and space. To read Lanark's adventures as hallucination confines Hell to that small area within Duncan Thaw's tormented psyche, whereas the whole point of the novel is that Hell is vast and we are in it. Unthank is Glasgow is the industrial, post-war world.

The institute, still running after having been set up during the war, represents a fragmenting of space and time, and Thaw's childhood world is fragmented in much the same way, and for the same reason. Book One begins with Chapter Twelve: 'The War Begins'. It's 1939 and Thaw's working-class family is evacuated from Glasgow. Thaw's view of the war is the view from boyhood: he can play at German spies on the beach and confidently announce to the local minister that he doesn't believe in Hell. To which Dr McPhedron prophetically replies: 'When you have more knowledge of life you will mibby find Hell more believable' (143). Young Thaw doesn't know it but Hell starts here and at a later date he will be able to point out its exact landmarks to his father:

> 'Look at Belsen!' cried Thaw. 'And Nagasaki, and the Russians in Hungary and Yanks in South America and French in Algeria and the British bombing Egypt without declaring war on her! Half the folk on this planet die of malnutrition before they're thirty, we'll be twice as many before the century ends, and the only governments with the skill and power to make a decent home of the world are plundering their neighbours and planning to atom bomb each other. We cooperate in millions when it comes to killing, but when it comes to generous, beautiful actions we work in tens and hundreds.' (295)

Social and industrial decline follow the war. Thaw's father can only find work as a labourer and his friends leave school for jobs which are boring, and dangerous: '. . . this business of being a *man* keeps you happy for mibby a week, then on your second Monday it hits you' (215). One half of the planet's population dies of malnutrition while the other half thrives: 'Men are pies that bake and eat themselves' (188). A metaphor that, in the institute, becomes fact; Lanark discovers that the patients who aren't cured are used as fuel and food, despite many sections of the institute being owned by decent people 'who don't know they are cannibals and wouldn't believe it if you told them' (102).

Lanark is a study of the way power, particularly political power, works, and how it is fuelled by greed, hate, separation, and the inability to love. When, in the Epilogue, Lanark encounters his maker, the author/conjurer Nastler, he is told that: 'The Thaw narrative shows a man dying because he is bad at loving. It is enclosed by your narrative which shows civilization collapsing for the same reason' (484). Thaw, the schoolboy who doesn't believe in Hell, goes on to become Thaw the adolescent, wracked with asthma and eczema and the awareness that 'Hell was the one truth and pain the one fact that nullified all others'

(160). Thaw the art student struggles against class, poverty, and an inflexible education system; but his most important failures are his own. He is a man who, like the society around him, is bad at loving. A man who, in his final breakdown, believes he has – and in fact might have – killed Marjory, the woman he loves but who doesn't love him back.

Duncan Thaw throws himself into the sea in 1956; toward the close of the century Lanark is an old man who has ventured into alternative worlds, and across time zones, in an unsuccessful attempt to save Unthank from destruction. Lanark's, however, is a different failure from Thaw's because, although inept and easily manipulated, he is capable of love. 'I never wanted anything', he tells Nastler, 'but some sunlight, some love, some very ordinary happiness' (484). He saves the life of Rima (once Marjory) in the institute, and is willing to risk his own life to save their son, Alexander. Love does triumph. And Alexander's existence confounds Lanark's creator:

> The conjuror stared and said, 'You have no son.'
> 'I have a son called Alexander who was born in the Cathedral.'
> (498)

Lanark's final chapter is simply entitled 'End'. Nastler warns his character that 'my whole imagination has a carefully reined-back catastrophic tendency' (498) and when Lanark demands to know what will happen to his son, his creator simply replies: 'I can't change my overall plan now. Why should I be kinder than my century? The millions of children who've been vilely murdered this century . . .' (498–99).

Time has run out. In Unthank people pay for what they need now by pledging their futures (437), and there is no future left: 'let us thrill the readers with a description of you ending in company. Let the ending be worldwide, for such a calamity is likely nowadays' (496). There is a promise of a catastrophe of biblical proportions, although at the last the immediate threat abates, leaving Lanark aware of his own approaching death but relatively at peace with himself: 'a slightly worried, ordinary old man but glad to see the light in the sky' (560). Around him, however, a war continues to rage and there is little doubt that Unthank will finally succumb, swallowed by the creature which is otherwise manifested in the power structures known as as the institute, the council, the foundation (409).

II

Where Alasdair Gray is a better writer than he sometimes seems, Martin Amis sometimes seems to be better a writer than he actually is. The most common criticism of Amis's work is that the parts are better than the whole, a contagious style ultimately failing to make up for lack of content. At the same time, there is no doubt that London Fields is both an indicator of the zeitgeist, as well as an influence, and no discussion of the millennium in contemporary British fiction can afford to leave it off the list.

Amis's text shares Lanark's sense of there not being much time left: 'Oh, Christ, no, the hell of time. . . . Time takes from you, with both hands. Things just disappear into it' (239). As the Note to London Fields explains, an alternative title could have been Millennium. However as 'M.A.' (the text is a prolonged tease and we're never sure whether we're in the hands of Martin Amis, real author, or Mark Asprey, fictional creation) explains: 'everything is called Millennium just now'. So London Fields it is: 'This book is called London Fields. London Fields . . .' [p. vii].

Although the year is supposed to be 1999, 1989 is how it reads, with the bubble of the Eighties about to burst and recession immediately around the corner. London is at crisis point – although it is difficult to identify what form the crisis will actually take. Certainly the weather is behaving very oddly, there are cyclonic winds (killing 'nineteen people, and thirty- three million trees' (43). The animals are dying (97), and rumour has it that there is to be massive flooding, cosmic rays, and the Second Coming (118). The natural world is on fastforward, rushing toward catastrophe with the political situation racing to keep up. There's danger of 'A flare-up. A flashpoint somewhere' (105). The international situation is mysteriously linked to the ill-health of Faith, the First Lady (207), and the 'new buzz word' is 'Cathartic war' (417). The sun is daily sinking lower as the earth tilts on its axis in anticipation of a full eclipse on November 5, at which point, so the rumours go, two nuclear bombs will explode, 'one over the Palace of Culture in Warsaw, one over Marble Arch' (394).

It's the end of the century and the planet is braced for impact (197) because while previous millenniums didn't really mean the end of the world ('Nobody had the hardware', 369), this time things are different. But when November 5 does come around, there isn't a bang but a whimper. The comet doesn't hit, the bombs don't explode, the sun returns to its normal position. A woman, however, is murdered and we are back with what we were promised on the novel's first page: 'This is the story of a murder.'

London Fields is a murder story, popular fiction dressed up as high art, a text that functions as much as a textbook (designed for the undergraduate seminar requiring neat examples of the metafictional and postmodern) as a novel. Where in Lanark there are 'two' novels, one an experiment in realism, the other science fiction, London Fields is also multi-layered, the commentary of the narrator, Samson Young, sandwiching the fiction he is writing. The commentary, of course, tells us that this fiction is 'real' ('This is a true story but I can't believe it's really happening,' 1): a woman – Nicola Six, 'the murderee' – dumps her diaries in a London rubbish bin (26) and an author finds a ready-made story. At the same time Nicola Six finds her murderer. Or, rather, potential murderer for while, in Lawrentian terms, a murderee is always a murderee, 'The murderer was not yet a murderer' (18). A murderer has to be made, and so Samson Young describes how Nicola goes to work on Keith Talent who, although 'a very bad guy', working class, petty crook, wife-beater, rapist, is not yet 'the very worst ever' (4). It is up to Nicola to turn him into that, and in order to transform Keith into what is required she plays him off against Guy Clinch – upper class, nice guy, handsome, rich (27).

Nicola Six (a blend of sex and an Apocalyptic 666) has from an early age always known 'what was going to happen next' (15), and in the case of her own murder is playing both prophet and author. Why she wants to die is another matter: 'It's what she's always wanted' (1). Nicola Six is a heart, and ball, breaker: 'She pauperized gigilos, she spayed studs, she hospitalized heartbreakers' (21). For Guy, Nicola plays the virgin, teasing him into a state whereby he loses dignity, sanity, family. For Keith she's the whore. Nicola is all things to all men: 'I'm worried', Samson Young tells her, 'they're going to say you're a male fantasy figure.' To which the reply is 'I am a male fantasy figure. I've been one for fifteen years. It really takes it out of a girl' (260).

If this is the writer (the real writer, Martin Amis) attempting to cover himself the attempt is less than a success. Geoff Dyer confides that 'youngish male writers' find themselves struggling against the influence of the Amis style ('. . . the guy has got it. I mean, really') and 'accusing each other of imitating him' (Dyer, 8). Some women critics, however, appear to find Amis less difficult to resist (Ellison, 21) and it is easy to see how the depiction of Nicola Six invites accusations of misogyny, even though Amis's apparent intention is for his female character to be read as a symbol of her age rather than a sign of her gender. Nicola is self-destructive, compelled not just to cancel love but to murder it (21), a perversion of emotion which, according to this text, is reflected in a predeliction for sodomy: 'It was the only thing about herself that she couldn't understand and wouldn't forgive' (67). But while Nicola can't quite comprehend her own desires she is aware that 'Literature *did* go on about sodomy, and increasingly' (67). Joyce, Lawrence, Beckett, Updike, Mailer, Roth, Naipaul (68), compiling her list of (male) writers she is tempted to see sodomy as a 'twentieth-century theme', and Nicola 'would be perfectly prepared to represent her century' (67–8). Sodomy, for Nicola, is about negation – '*That's what I am*, she used to whisper to herself after sex. A *black hole. Nothing can escape from me.*' (67) – and that too is the motto of the suicidal last century of the second millennium.

The twentieth century has 'come along and after several try-outs and test-drives it put together an astonishing new offer: death for everybody . . .' (297). At the end, however, death calls only for Nicola, who barely whimpers. This doesn't mean that the big bang won't happen, but is more a recognition that it has happened already. We've already seen the big one, and are living in its aftermath. The big one was the Second World War and what it unleashed, the possibility of nuclear holocaust. Just as Nicola has known since childhood what was going to happen next she's been accompanied by an invisible companion: '. . . Enola Gay. Enola wasn't real. Enola came from inside the head of Nicola Six' (16). As part of her effort to humiliate Guy, Nicola extracts large amounts of money from him on the pretext of trying to save Enola Gay and her little boy, stranded in south-east Asia as a result of the Cambodian war. But just as Enola Gay isn't really a refugee in Thailand or Burma, she isn't a fantasy either:

> 'Enola Gay' was the plane that flew the mission to Hiroshima. The pilot named the aircraft after his mother. He was once her little boy. But Little Boy was the name of the atom bomb. It killed 50,000 people in 120 seconds. (445)

Nicola has been able to con Guy because, like the vast majority, he hasn't known one of the most important facts in his sad century's history. Similarly, Keith has to be told that the bikini Nicola dons is named after the Bikini Atoll:

> 'What American men did there – one of the greatest crimes in human history. If you got the world's most talented shits and cruelty experts together, they couldn't come up with anything worse than Bikini. And how do we commemorate the crime, Keith?' She indicated the

two small pieces of her two-piece. 'Certain women go about wearing this trash. It's very twentieth-century, don't you think?'
   'Yeah. Diabolical.' (127)

So diabolical in fact that it's as if the Second World War never really ended: '. . . it seemed possible to argue that Hitler was still running the century. Hitler, the great bereaver' (395). History ended mid-century and what we are caught in in *London Fields* is the hell of the perpetual present.

Nicola Six, the murderee, walks in the shadow of Enola Gay, and so too does her murderer. When Nicola appears in the Black Cross pub Samson Young leaps to the conclusion that she's recognized her murderer in Keith. But this is one of those whodunnits in which the unwitting narrator turns out to be the 'who'. 'She leaned forward. "You," she said, with intense recognition. "Always you . . ." ' (465). Nicola had known him from the start (466). And Young should have known too because he and Nicola are linked by the fact that they're both as good as dead already (260). However where Nicola, representative of a self-destructive century, wills her own death, Young has had his willed on him as a legacy of the work his father did, in London Fields, on High Explosives Research (120, 161).

Samson Young is 'pre-nuked and dead-already' (323). So when Guy is about to kill Nicola, Young can make a deal with him and take his place because he has nothing to lose. 'After the first blow she gave a moan of visceral assent' (467) and the narrator is left to take a suicide pill. A murder and a suicide and everything goes back to normal. Which is the problem with *London Fields* because, ultimately, any political message there is about the destructive temperament of the century, the madness of things nuclear, is lost as the skies clear and the novel, like other of Amis's novels, concludes by valorizing class and gender (Doan, 79). The woman gets what she's asking for and her death is, ultimately, engineered by Guy who beats up the already-humiliated Keith and reasserts himself as the dominant, upper-class male. The post-war, postmodern, postmillennial world gets back to normal.

III

Hannah Arendt's explorations of the dynamics of holocaust have demonstrated the banality of evil, and this is the premise behind Shena Mackay's powerful, and alarming novel, *Dunedin*. Mackay's text begins as a realist novel set in 1909, effortlessly jumps forward into a dark comedy about middle-class, suburban life in south London, 1989, then skews sideways into a surreal, alternative world which serves as a nightmarish vision of the future.

In the early years of the new century the minister Jack Mackenzie and his family, fresh from Scotland, sail into Dunedin harbour, New Zealand, and find: 'the New World glittering at the end of the beams which streamed from the fingers of God as a sign that all would be well' (3). In this last century of the second millennium, however, God's influence is decidedly weak. Jack Mackenzie, hypocrite and sensualist, disregards the needs of his flock, tyrannises over his family, and is more interested in science than religion. Nothing is well at all.

Where cause and effect are tenuous in both *Lanark* and *London Fields*, the equation is carefully worked out in *Dunedin*. Thus Sandy, Jack Mackenzie's son, will become overtly what his father is covertly, a professional con-man. The minister brings bad luck on his son, and on his son's children, the Mackenzie family representing in miniature the repercussions of imperialism and colonialism on future generations. When they leave Dunedin they take bad luck with them back to the Old World in the form of a preserved head which Jack steals – as a scientific curiosity – from his Maori lover, Myrtille. But the head is '*tapu* . . . sacred or magic' (27): in 1811 a sailor stole a similar one and six years later was killed, along with some of his shipmates, by the natives he'd robbed. In revenge the Maori city of Otago was set alight and destroyed (10–11). Jack Mackenzie knows the story, but doesn't heed its lesson.

Eighty years later the English, once with a mighty empire to exploit, can only exploit each other. South London in 1989 is, like the rest of Europe, a frightening and dangerous place where it is no longer safe to let children play in the park alone (60). A fact recognized only too well by William Mackenzie, Jack Mackenzie's grandson, whose career as a headmaster comes to an end when one of his students is murdered on a school trip. William blames himself:

> almost every moment of the day and night, waking screaming in a sodden, strangling tangle of sheets. The horror of the child's going.
> (61)

It is for their lost children that William and his sister, Olive, grieve. Olive finds a solution in the simple expedient of child-napping. The pretty black baby in his mother's arms on the tube is irresistible and when Olive gets him back home she announces that he is named

Theodore: the next morning her brother leaves this 'Gift of God' (81)
outside a local hospital.

Olive sees the baby as a desirable object; less desirable is the scruffy
boy she meets in the Horniman Museum. Nineteen-year-old Jay Pascal,
newly arrived from New Zealand, is beaten and robbed on his arrival
in London (280), and is appalled by the 'vastness, noise and dirt' of the
city (66). Should she ask him, Jay – who might not be a gift from God
but is certainly one of God's holy fools – would be only too happy to go
and live in Olive's house. But all Olive offers is a lift, and even when
he asks to be dropped off at 'Dunedin', once the Mackenzie family home
but now a derelict squat, she fails to ask why this young New Zealander
has come to stay at this particular address. If she did ask she would
discover that Jay, brought up in an orphanage in New Zealand, has made
his way 'home': Jack Mackenzie not only stole the sacred head from
Myrtille, but left her pregnant, and Jay is his great-grandson.

Jay soon joins the ranks of the 'ruined people' (70). This is the
wasteland of the Eighties, the Thatcher years: the hospitals and asylums
are in the process of being demolished and the patients have been left
to make their own way in 'what they had been taught to call the
community' (73). The disaffected, deranged, and dispossessed, sleep in
doorways, beg at tube stations – and it is at this point that Mackay's
vision of the future begins to shape itself along the lines of what is, after
all, not a remote past. Because before long:

> There were those who had decided that something must be done
> about them. Private enterprise was engaged to trawl the streets in the
> dead hours before dawn. . . . Rumours of disappearances circulated
> in crypts and park benches and in derelict houses but nobody walked
> into a police station to register a vagrant as a missing person.
>
> (73–4)

The reality of late-Eighties England, the increase in begging and
homelessness, the well-publicized moves to 'clean up' areas like the
Strand and the cardboard city clustered around the South Bank,
reverberates with the reality of late-Thirties Nazi Germany. The millennium is on the doorstep and its shape is that of the Holocaust, the
'T4' euthenasia programme and the removal of 'asocials' to concentration, and death, camps.

Late one night Jay is bundled into a windowless van 'marked Depart-
ment of the Environment' (187) and finds himself at St Anne's, a vast
Victorian house which has quietly been removed from the Ordnance
Survey maps and isn't listed in the telephone book: 'it was as if it did

not exist' (185). And the people who have been brought here, 'herded into the reek of misery and rot', might as well not exist any longer either:

> They were being addressed by a man in a quasi-uniform of navy blue: '. . . and just in case there should be any barrack-room lawyers among you, with any fancy ideas about Human Rights, I should point out that you lot have renounced any claim you might once have had to humanity. You are no longer human beings. You are the scum of the earth. Your subsciptions to Amnesty International have been cancelled. If you have any friends, which I very much doubt, they won't find you here. Oh yes, one more thing, there is no way out, so don't even think about it.' (188)

This is the discourse of power and brutality, legitimized as 'the Vagrancy Act' (318), and in the face of this Jay's appeal for justice on behalf of himself and his fellow prisoners is not only futile but dangerous: 'Why am I being kept prisoner here? And it's not just me, all of us, we haven't committed any crimes and if we had we're entitled to a hearing, not just to be locked up and beaten . . .' (318). A sign above a row of bins reads 'Refuse To Be Incinerated', which is how the institution's staff regard the inmates. Jay reads the same sign and determines to survive: 'I will refuse . . . I am still myself. I won't let them destroy me. I will get out of here' (236).

The reader is tantalized with the hope that Jay might escape the incinerators. Father Jeremy, a vicar who in these last days of the century cherishes a touching faith in God, also harbours the suspicion that something is dreadfully wrong at St Anne's: 'I know that God wants me to find out what it is' (193). He eventually hears the truth from the director's secretary:

> As Cheryl spoke of vans disgorging broken people into the court-yard, of black-windowed private ambulances, the secret laboratories, locked rooms where naked men and women rocked silently in filth, the faint far-off cries of children, it was as though a troop of demons streamed from those rosebud lips. (315)

Jeremy, blessed with a loving wife, a baby son, and the ability sometimes to read others' thoughts, seems to be just the person to blow Dr Barrables' establishment sky-high. This is the conclusion that Barrables comes to himself, with the result that Olive later reads about: 'a curate and his family, wife and child, who had been killed in a freak accident, when their Volkswagen Beetle had run off a seemingly empty country road in broad daylight and somersaulted down a chalky bank (326).

'Hell on Earth', Olive reads in her paper, 'Greek Island of the Insane Exposed. Why it couldn't happen here . . .' (325). But Hell is here already, experienced by 'a monkey with . . . tubes and electrodes coming out of his scalped head' (193), 'galvanised animal concentration camps set in stinking yards' (265). It is only a short step from here to the conclusion that if people like Jay are 'no longer human beings' (188) then genocide is, *humane*. Like with animals . . . the kindest thing . . .' (241).

Olive, wrapped in her cloak of self-centred, middle-class *angst*, can read the newspaper article about the dead curate and his family without reading it: ' "They'll be all right," she thought dully, turning the page' (326). Passing a boy huddled outside a pub she does briefly remember Jay and 'if goodwill had any power against evil a spark flared for a second in the darkness' (329). But in the gathering gloom that is the end of the second millennium, evil has won out and for Olive the only answer left is a return to the God that her grandfather turned his back on at the beginning of the century: ' "Well," she thought. "Seeing as no one else bloody well wants me, I'd better see if God will take me back" ' (330). In this black comedy this might either be a reference to suicide, or to the Evangelicals who have just passed by.

The suggestion of suicide links Olive to Thaw/Lanark, and Samson Young. However a stronger link among *Dunedin*, *Lanark*, and *London Fields*, is the fear we feel not so much for ourselves but for our children, and our anxiety that they should be kept safe. In *Dunedin* successive generations fail their children and in the last years of the century there is no assurance that anyone can keep a child safe. However the one sliver of hope that the novel does offer is the fact that Olive's brother, William, has found a lover and conceived a child.

As Nastler reminds Lanark, this is a century in which millions of children have been vilely murdered. Lanark, a child of the Second World War, is desperate to know what will happen to his son Alexander in the war which is to engulf Unthank. And Alexander, in turn, is quick to assure Lanark that his own daughter is 'in a safer place than this, thank goodness' (556). Meanwhile, in *London Fields*, Nicola Six is finally murdered for the sake of a child. Samson Young loves Keith's baby daughter, Kim. Kim, however, is being abused by her mother, Kath, who is abused by Keith. The deal Young strikes with Guy means that Kath and Kim will be looked after financially, and Kim will be safe in the future.

With the Second World War history entered hell's gates, and never came out again. Apocalypse but with no Second Coming, no heavenly jurisdiction. But while history might have ended some fifty years ago it is still possible to hope that it can move forward once again through future generations. Thus, as the sun sets on the battleground that was the twentieth century time becomes even more urgent, for it is now: 'time to do this, time to look for our children and see how many we can find' (*London Fields*, 469).

Works Cited

Amis, Martin, 1990 (1989). *London Fields*, Penguin.
Doan, Laura L., 1990. ' "Sexy Greedy *Is* the Late Eighties": Power Systems in Amis's *Money* and Churchill's *Serious Money*,' *Minnesota Review* 34–5, Spring-Fall, 69–80.
Dyer, Geoff, 1993. 'Mad about the boy,' *The Guardian*, 2 Nov., 8.
Ellison, Jane, 1989. 'Battlefields,' *The Guardian*, 12 Oct., 21.
Gifford, Douglas, 1987. 'Private Confession and Public Satire in the Fiction of Alasdair Gray,' *Chapman* 10.i and ii, Summer, 101–16.
Gray, Alasdair, 1991 (1981). *Lanark*, Picador.
Imhoff, Rudiger, 1990. 'Chinese Box: Flann O'Brien in the Metafiction of Alasdair Gray, John Fowles, and Robert Coover,' *Eire-Ireland* 25.i, Spring, 64–79.
Lee, Alison, 1990. 'Un-mastering masterful images,' in *Realism and Power: Postmodern British Fiction*, Routledge, 99–127.
Mackay, Shena, 1992. *Dunedin*, Penguin.
O'Toole, Fintan, 1995. 'The Dredd of 2000 AD,' *The Guardian*, 7 Jan., 29.

Last Days: Millennial Hysteria
in Don DeLillo's Mao II

JEREMY GREEN

THE APOCALYPTIC IMAGINATION sees in unconnected events the coherent signs of an ending. Whether such signs portend a cataclysm followed by a rebirth, or point to an irreversible and rapid decline, the apocalyptic imagination interprets history in accordance with categories drawn from theology or metaphysics. For the American novelist Don DeLillo, news of catastrophe and disaster lends an apocalyptic tenor to everyday life, hinting at the presence of a dark and meaningful narrative behind the humdrum contingencies of the quotidian. Throughout his career, DeLillo has been an acute analyst of the dread and appeal of worst-case scenarios, opening up the prose of his novels to the chatter and chic of contemporary anxieties. Even a cursory glance at his fiction will reveal a panorama of American fears spanning the last thirty years and more: nuclear war, random violence, conspiracy, assassination, ecological disaster – the list is an extensive one. But, in addition, DeLillo's characters are informed by a sense that it might well be preferable to resort to extreme solutions, rather than continue to endure the randomness they find in their environments. Here lies the appeal of conspiracies and apocalyptic narratives, manic games and extreme forms of asceticism and violence. In DeLillo's 1991 novel, *Mao II*, a minor character sums up the contemporary sensibility as one characterized by 'inertia-hysteria' (157). What sort of psychological coupling is this? Inertia indicates a collapse on the part of the subject, the retreat into a kind of stunned indifference, a response typical of many of DeLillo's characters when faced with a volume of information – a whole hypertrophic culture of news, celebrity and catastrophe – which exceeds their capacity for assimilation. To the numbed and weary subject distinctions appear blurred, categories muddled, hierarchies overturned. In discourses celebratory of postmodernism, confusion of this kind may be seen as a novel freedom, a heady release from the tyranny of metaphysics; but such disorientation – for DeLillo's characters at any rate – is moral as well as psychological. The uncertainty is one of scale and perspective; it ceases to be clear what is important, what trivial. Responses to this condition in DeLillo's work often involve a jump to the other extreme – the hysteria of ardent belief

129

and extreme action, an obliteration of self in heightened states of consciousness.

This sensibility of 'inertia-hysteria', moving between melancholy and mania, may be seen as one engaged in a struggle to cope without credible narratives. A number of influential accounts of postmodernism – notably those of Fredric Jameson (1991) and Jean-François Lyotard (1984) – see the question of narrative, its uncertain survival or felicitous demise, as a central one for contemporary theory and politics. In *Mao II* the narratives concern art, politics and the relation between them. A number of recognisably postmodern themes – the death of the author, the fate of high literary culture, the supposed twilight of ideology – converge with a set of anxieties that have emerged in the wake of a specific historical narrative, namely the Cold War. *Mao II* constellates these concerns around a series of motifs and figures – a reclusive novelist (who resembles Thomas Pynchon or J.D. Salinger) and a terrorist group, the individual and the crowd, celebrity culture and political iconicity. The danger here – and it is not one that *Mao II* entirely avoids – is the problem of excessive schematism: the complicated textures of the writing have a tendency to be resolved reductively into stark oppositions, and DeLillo's characteristically balanced ambiguities can on occasion degenerate into dubious conflations. In an important new study, *Late Imperial Romance* (1994), John McClure has traced these problems with *Mao II* to a disturbing tendency to make a scapegoat of Islamic fundamentalism for a crisis of meaning located in America's own self-understanding. For McClure, *Mao II* thus marks the return of an old and dishonourable narrative, that of imperialism. This is a grave charge, and it is not one I will directly contest in the present essay.[1] Instead, my focus in this analysis will be on the emergence of the crowd in *Mao II*. Fear of the crowd is the hallmark of an influential and strikingly resilient apocalyptic narrative, typified by Gustave Le Bon's characteristically ominous remark: 'Certainly it is possible that the advent to power of the masses marks one of the last stages of Western civilisation, a complete return to those periods of confused anarchy

[1] McClure's analysis, rightly in my view, draws attention to the ethnocentric bias of the novel, but it fails to consider the more complicated and compelling features of the text, which turn on the question of the special kind of crowd DeLillo tries to imagine, and which cast doubt on the conclusion that *Mao II* depicts 'America as the leader of a global crusade for democracy' (McClure, 150). As I try to show, the concept of democracy in the novel is rendered profoundly problematic.

which seem always destined to precede the birth of every new society'
(Le Bon, 17). While some of the perspectives offered on the crowds in
Mao II reproduce the terms of Le Bon's highly influential and reactionary crowd psychology, with its stress on the uniformity and contagion
of the group mind, DeLillo's crowds also have a more intriguing and
novel aspect that casts light on a number of questions concerning the
politics of the spectacle, the appeal of the apocalypse and the status of
the subject in a culture saturated with mass media images.

I

Mao II sets its forebodings into a slogan: 'The future belongs to crowds'
(16). This phrase is placed at the end of a charged description of a mass
Moonie wedding, which forms the prologue to the novel, and strikes
the portentous and minatory note that prevails for much of the book.
This first sequence, entitled 'At Yankee Stadium', bears only an oblique
relation to the novel's central narrative, but it forcefully establishes an
apocalyptic tone, and introduces the extremes of disbelief and certainty
with which the text will grapple. If the force of DeLillo's slogan is to be
assessed, and its implications worked out, it is with the spectacle of the
Moonie wedding that the analysis must begin. *Mao II* dwells at length
on a number of contemporary crowds, including the spectators crushed
in the Hillsborough disaster, the mourners at the Ayatollah Khomeini's
funeral and the protesters at Tiananmen Square, but these sequences
all fall to a greater or lesser extent under the shadow of the Moonie
crowd. The novel invites the reader to see the mass-marriage as the
image of an unthinkable future.

Such an invitation is, in a sense, an ironic inversion of this crowd's
assigned purpose. The mass-marriage is not a characteristic crowd, since
it does not gather in response to a particular occasion or strong emotion,
but involves instead both theatrical and religious impulses. The ceremony serves to unite six and a half thousand couples as part of the
global family of the Unification Church, and in so doing looks forward
to the redeemed time when the whole world will be organised as just
such a special kind of crowd. For the true believer this represents
humankind's salvation. For the non-believer, seeing in the spectacle
uniformity, repetition, credulousness, and the loss of selfhood, the
mass-marriage conjures up a nightmarish picture of the future.

But the Moonie ceremony is also unthinkable in a more immediate
and perceptual sense. Although it provokes many of the more obvious,

commonplace responses – the Moonies are 'fuelled by credulousness',
they reduce knowledge to 'a set of ready-made terms and empty repe-
titions' (7), they drill all individuality out of the faithful – the spectacle
in Yankee Stadium proves very difficult to comprehend, moving the
spectators both to awe and bewilderment, to astonishment and to a
kind of affective confusion, an uncertainty about what to feel. The
Moonie Karen's father Rodge, watching in the stands, is galvanized into
frantic action: he announces his intention to find helpline numbers, to
scour libraries and join support groups. Her mother, by contrast, appears
to lapse into an inertia alleviated only by a sardonic heartlessness: she
proposes they take in a play or a show. The parents in the stands make
an effort to defuse the impact of the spectacle by taking photographs,
'snapping anxiously, trying to shape a response or organize a memory,
trying to neutralize the event, drain it of eeriness and power' (6).
Snapshots hold out the promise of an eventual understanding, even as
they register a present incapacity. In part, the parents are struggling
with the shock of seeing the familiar made strange. Rodge reflects:
'There is a strangeness down there he never thought he'd see in a
ballpark. They take a time-honored event and repeat it, repeat it, repeat
it until something new enters the world' (4). What kind of new thing
is this? 'He works his glasses across the mass, the crowd, the movement,
the membership, the flock, the following' (5). The enumeration of
these near synonyms reflects an awareness of the different connotations
they carry, and testifies to Rodge's inability to give a name to what he
sees: ' "crowd" is not the right word. He doesn't know what to call them'
(4). What he sees, what he fails to name, is the many resolved into the
one, multiplicity into unity, the conversion of the individual participants into a shaped whole: 'From a series of linked couples they become
one continuous wave . . . one body now, an undifferentiated mass' (3).
This undifferentiated mass is 'turned into a sculptured object. It is like
a toy with thirteen thousand parts, just tootling along, an innocent and
menacing thing' (7). Unity appears in this simile as unthinking mechanical potency, the impassivity and motion of an automaton, an
image of the human transformed through sheer number into the
machine. The mechanical appearance the crowd assumes relates to
what is perhaps its most alarming, unthinkable aspect – the way in
which all that is cherished as intimate and private is rendered by the
ceremony crudely formulaic and public. This, finally, is what 'knocks
him back in awe, the loss of scale and intimacy, the way love and sex
are multiplied out' (7). Rodge's awe stems from the difficulty of imagining a self constituted in such a public and collective fashion, a

subjectivity devoid of any private space in which to formulate and express its inner needs. It is as if public space, or, more accurately, the space of the Unification Church, has collapsed into the private, subjective realm. The crowd erases particular identities, and implies a threat even to the identity of the spectators, who lose their cognitive and emotional bearings.

Searching the massed ranks with his binoculars, Rodge hopes to see his daughter, not because he imagines reclaiming her, at least not then and there, but because he will be reassured if he sees her that there remains something irreducibly particular about who she is: 'Healthy, intelligent, twenty-one, serious-sided, possessed of a selfness, a teeming soul, nuance and shadow, grids of pinpoint singularities they will never drill out of her' (7). The loss of selfhood that participation in the crowd involves is conveyed in two different ways. Selfhood, or, more accurately, individuality, is associated, first, with 'free will and independent thought' (7), which is termed in shorthand 'the language of self' (8). And, secondly, it is associated with the burden of corporeality. To join the crowd is to lose that burden: 'They're forgetting who they are under their clothes, leaving behind all the small banes and body woes, the daylong list of sore gums and sweaty nape and need to pee, ancient rumbles in the gut, momentary chill and tics' (8) – and so on, a lengthy catalogue of physical ailments and sorry particulars. The Moonie brides and grooms are described, in other words, as losing the specifics of their physical state and becoming a single organism, a unified body and collective subject. Master Moon is designated 'their true father' (6), and this description, which applies to his status in Unification Church doctrine as 'Lord of the Second Advent' (15) and leader of the world family, is developed as a biological metaphor, playing on the notion of genetic imprinting: 'They know him at molecular level. He lives in them like chains of matter that determine who they are' (6). Equally, a collective consciousness flows through the 'columned body' (7) of the Moonie crowd, expanding the participant perceptions of the individuals.

Karen sees Master Moon 'with the single floating eye of the crowd, inseparable from her own apparatus of vision but sharper-sighted, able to perceive more deeply. She feels intact, rayed with well-being' (7–8). Here the crowd is conceived as a single consciousness, unified through the senses, which sees the Master and returns the joyful sight to its own being, a felicitous, unbroken circuit, that makes sensory and spiritual vision one and the same. As such, the conceit is strikingly reminiscent of one of Emerson's best known passages: 'Standing on the bare ground,

– my head bathed by the blithe air, and uplifted into infinite space, – all mean egotism vanishes. I become a transparent eye-ball; I am nothing; I see all; the currents of the Universal Being circulate through me; I am part or particle of God' (Emerson, 6). This echo – witting or not – indicates the extent to which the events at Yankee Stadium are a challenge to a national as well as a personal identity. A part of the anxiety the mass-marriage incites in the spectators is the sense of the familiar space of a baseball stadium – Yankee Stadium – being occupied by a scene distinctly at odds with what is familiar and known, comfortably American. At one point during the ceremony, Karen turns to her Korean 'husband-for-eternity' (8) and says the word 'baseball', intending thereby 'to sum up a hundred happy abstractions, themes that flare to life in the crowd shout and diamond symmetry, in the details of a dusty slide' (8–9). The word 'baseball', the reader is told, 'has resonance if you're American, a sense of shared heart and untranslatable lore' (9). But a crowd shout and shared heart of quite a different kind have come to occupy and make strange the stadium and all its warm associations, displacing the themes and details that comprise in baseball a symbolic form through which national identity may be represented and performatively enacted. American identity, the subtext implies, is warm, gregarious and passionate, and is not something that can be learned by rote or impressed by brainwashing. Such an implication proves ironically unfounded in the course of the novel: Karen is later seized on the street and subjected to days of repetitive 'deprogramming' to turn her back into a good, middle-class American, a contented citizen of the 'land of lawns' (9).

The prologue comes to its ominous climax with two different perspectives on the Moonies' crowd shout. By chanting, the Moonie crowd makes the world coincide with itself – 'the chant becomes the boundaries of the world' (15) – absorbing personal contingencies, and subsuming differences of individual and national identity in a final, all-consuming plea:

> They are gripped by the force of a longing. They know at once, they feel it, all of them together, a longing deep in time, running in the earthly blood. This is what people have wanted since consciousness became corrupt. The chant brings the End Time closer. The chant is the End Time. They feel the power of the human voice, the power of the single word repeated as it moves them into oneness. They chant for world-shattering rapture, for the truth of prophecies and astonishments. They chant for new life, peace eternal, the end of soul-lonely pain. Someone on the bandstand beats a massive drum.

They chant for one language, one word, for the time when names are lost. (16)

In this passage, the relationship between the crowd and millennial desire is unequivocally asserted. The appeal of the crowd, and of the Moon system which centres (in *Mao II*, at any rate) on the establishment of a global crowd, is seen here as an atavistic longing to abolish all kinds of separations and distinctions – cultural, psychological and linguistic. The intersection of redemptive and linguistic motifs is common to a number of DeLillo's characters, offering in this instance a release into a mass unity which many of those same characters seldom fail to find both appealing and horrifying.[2] The kind of unity imagined here is one purchased at the highest possible cost. In chanting their way into a final, unimaginable oneness, the Moonies turn the desire for the interpersonal and the collective, for loving familial but also benign social relations, into a cataclysmic erasure of the identities that would sustain any mutuality. For the genuinely collective does not imply a refusal of identity, but a way of mediating between differences, sharing what is common while respecting the distinctiveness of what is not. Bill Gray's remarks, reported by his amanuensis, Scott, provide the most pungent commentary:

> Mass-married. Married in a public ceremony involving thousands of others. Bill calls it millennial hysteria. By compressing a million moments of love and touch and courtship into one accelerated mass, you're saying that life must become more anxious, more surreal, more image-bound, more prone to hurrying its own transformation, or what's the point? You take marriage, the faith of the species, the means of continuation, and you turn it into catastrophe, a total implosion of the future. Quoting Bill. (80)

These assertions provide a significant cue, even though they do not go unchallenged, hinting that the ceremony at Yankee Stadium should be

---

[2] The foremost example is Owen Brademas, the archaeologist and student of ancient scripts, who is simultaneously drawn to and repelled by the *Hadj*. His obsession with the form of letters is intimately related to his sense of the boundaries of his own subjectivity; the running crowd of the pilgrimage to Mecca threatens those boundaries with what he sees as a 'whirlwind of human awe and submission' (*The Names*, 296). This prospect is consistently likened in the novel to his early experiences as a frightened member of a Pentecostalist congregation that spoke in tongues.

understood not simply and reductively as aberrant or bizarre, but as a commentary on a certain contemporary sensibility, presenting not an unaccountable, alien event, but more, much more, of the same, a common set of anxieties and perceptions in an extraordinarily public form. Anxious, surreal, image-bound, hungry for transformation – these are to be seen as the prominent aspects of contemporary millennialism, aspects that provide the focus and much of the tone of DeLillo's writing.

In the present discussion, however, I want to concentrate on what is perhaps the most significant of these characteristics – 'image-bound'. The construction indicates a claustrophobic prevalence of images, hinting that the image is what entraps us, besets us, bogs us down; but the phrase might also carry connotations of binding as connecting, tying, or joining, perhaps implying that the image is what links people, binds them socially. Such implications may well include too the suggestion of helotry. This opens up a different perspective on the mass-marriage. For the ceremony is not just a convenient way to join simultaneously six and a half thousand couples in matrimony, it is also an extraordinary photo-opportunity.[3] From within the Moonie crowd, Karen notes the presence of another crowd: 'She's close enough to the grandstand to see people crowding the rails, standing everywhere to take pictures. Did she ever think she'd find herself in a stadium in New York, photographed by thousands of people?' (10). The rhetorical question attributed to Karen is a near-echo of her father's own bewilderment ('There is a strangeness down there he never thought he'd see in a ballpark' [4]), suggesting that the peculiarity of the event is not confined to the field but encompasses too the thousands of parents with their cameras. Rodge's astonishment at seeing the familiar-made-strange has its counterpart in Karen's recognition of her curious celebrity; she is photographed, in effect, thousands of times, like a famous ball-player, but the cameras will only capture her as a tiny figure indistinguishable from the surrounding multitude. 'There may be as many people taking pictures as there are brides and grooms. One of them for every one of us' (10), Karen muses. The couples have the sensation that '[t]hey're here but also there, already in the albums and slide projectors, filling picture frames with their microcosmic bodies, the minikin selves they are trying to become' (10). The best representation of a subjectivity attuned to the crowd turns out, surprisingly

---

[3] DeLillo has revealed how his idea for *Mao II* evolved from two newspaper images: a snapshot of a very alarmed J.D. Salinger and a picture of a Moonie wedding (Evans).

enough, to be the photographic image. And the transparency or print in its slide projector or family album proves to be as much the destiny, the future, towards which these faithful brides and grooms aspire as the loudly chanted End Time invoked at the ceremony's climax, whether they know it or not.[4] For this reason, Rodge's unlikely vision of the crowd at the culmination of the mass-marriage may be just as apt as Karen's own: 'He half expects the chanting mass of bodies to rise in the air, all thirteen thousand ascending slowly to the height of the stadium roof, lifted by the picture-taking, the forming of aura, radiant brides clutching their bouquets, grooms showing sunny teeth' (15). Far from neutralizing the event, 'drain[ing] it of eeriness and power' (6), the massed cameras in the stadium, one for each of the participants if Karen is right, are in fact an integral part of that eeriness and power. For the photographic image mediates the ceremony from beginning to end, from the moment prior to the marriage when the couples are selected by matching snapshots (as later becomes clear [183]), to the final imagined exaltation of the crowd as image. In this respect, the uniformity which is said to characterise the Moonie crowd may have as much to do with technologies of reproduction as with notions of rote-learning and brainwashing. And, in much the same way, that other familar metaphor for crowd behaviour, contagion or viral contiguity, is reworked to suit the spatial effects of photography: 'They feel that space is contagious' (10). Notwithstanding the prologue's emphasis on religious fervour and irrationality, it is important to see the Moonie mass-marriage as both an apocalyptic tableau, in which the couples marching to 'the end of human history' (6) bear some relation to the 'miles of delirium' (7) outside the stadium (whether this relation is conceived as symptomatic in some way or as the common sensibility writ large), and, at the same time, as an exemplary postmodern spectacle, an event dedicated to the production of what DeLillo calls 'aura'.

To acquire a better sense of what DeLillo intends to convey by the term 'aura', it is necessary to move forward to Karen's reappearance in the novel as a member of Bill Gray's household. Although no longer a Moonie in any strict sense, she retains the qualities that marked her as a subject of the crowd; she is still highly impressionable, uncannily open to whatever claims may be made on her attention and belief, both peculiarly affectless and given to extreme emotion. These qualities are

---

[4] One of the novel's ironies is that the reader's last glimpse of the arch-individualist Bill Gray is his photographic image, reproduced many times on a set of contact prints, appearing like 'mass visual litter that occupies a blink' (222).

no longer placed in the radiant sway of Master Moon, but are tuned instead to the luminous images emanating from the television set. Her participation in the spectacle may be more prosaic in this second incarnation, but it is no less unyielding:

> She watched the set at the foot of the bed . . . her eyes sweeping the screen. She was thin-boundaried. She took it all in, she believed it all, pain, ecstasy, dog food, all the seraphic matter, the baby bliss that falls from the air. Scott stared at her and waited. She carried the virus of the future. Quoting Bill. (119)

For Karen, the TV screen offers a stream of variegated materials – pain, ecstasy, dog food – which all apparently carry the charge of revealed truth, 'seraphic matter'.[5] Rapt and indiscriminate her viewing may be, but she is still particularly drawn to news footage of crowds, as perhaps befits one infected with the 'virus of the future'. In the course of the novel, she watches news footage of a number of recent events involving crowds, the first instance being the Hillsborough disaster. With the volume turned down, the televisual presentation turns the horrific event into a strangely artful vision of torment: 'She sees the fence close up and they stop the film and it is like a religious painting, the scene could be a fresco in a tourist church, it is composed and balanced and filled with people suffering' (33). The technology and conventions of television disaster coverage conspire to turn the event into a scene or spectacle, an object of contemplation, at the touch of a button.

But why is the resulting freeze-frame likened to a fresco in a tourist church? An argument concerning the changing place and function of cultural artefacts is implicit in the simile DeLillo adopts.[6] The comparison is emphatic: as Karen watches, '[t]hey show the fence from a distance, bodies piling up behind it, smothered, sometimes only

---

5   In this respect, Karen's viewing habits are faithful to the theory of television propounded by the popular culture professor Murray Jay Siskind in *White Noise*. For Siskind, the televisual medium 'practically overflows with sacred formulas if we can remember how to respond innocently and get past our irritation, weariness and disgust' (*White Noise*, 51).
6   The argument in this paragraph adapts that of Walter Benjamin in 'The Work of Art in the Age of Mechanical Reproduction'. DeLillo has given an indication of the significance of the Benjamin essay for his work in a television documentary (Evans). For some comments on the relation between the Benjamin essay and *White Noise*, see John Frow's article ' "The Last Things Before the Last": Notes on *White Noise*'.

fingers moving, and it is like a fresco in an old dark church, a crowded twisted vision of a rush to death as only a master of the age could paint it' (34). When a 'master of the age' paints a fresco on a church wall, a vision of the last judgement, perhaps, or a menacing glimpse of the agonies of the damned, the image will play its part as an object of devotion, instruction and veneration in a complex religious, cultural and social formation. The fresco will participate in a tradition of sacred meanings, assuming a primacy in the spiritual life of a people which its temporal and spatial uniqueness does nothing to dispel. But when the fresco becomes in turn the focus of a different kind of contemplative attention, that of the tourist, who visits the 'old dark church' not to worship but as a part of a cultural consumer's itinerary, its social and cultural significance may be said to have changed. The painting is now venerated as a work of art, as a repository of aesthetic values; its religious significance recedes. At this juncture, the role of the painter assumes a new importance, and the fresco comes to be valued not just for its aesthetic qualities, but also for its status as the authentic work of a master, an expression of the unique psychic, or quasi-divine, constitution of the genius. In likening the news footage to a work in a 'tourist church', the work of a 'master of the age', DeLillo evokes not just the visual qualities of the television image, but also the cultural and social framing of the fresco. Television reframes the objects of its attention, translating them from event into spectacle, aestheticizing and objectifying that which it reports, records and witnesses, turning live coverage into iconic image. By the same token, the icons that television produces have a centrality, a primacy and significance, to contemporary culture that is comparable to the work of a 'master of the age', not only because the events captured by the coverage are themselves of the greatest significance (the 'real' significance of events and the significance they are accorded by the mass media will not in any case prove separable), but also because the images themselves dominate the imagination, acquiring an instantaneous aesthetic resonance that is no longer available to works of art.

For Walter Benjamin, in 'The Work of Art in the Age of Mechanical Reproduction', the movement from venerated art object to reproducible image entails the destruction of what he termed 'aura', since the meaning attached to the uniqueness of the original undergoes a profound shift with the emergence of new technologies of reproduction.[7]

---

[7] Benjamin's concept of aura is a complicated and equivocal one, reflecting the roots of his work in German Idealism. On the definition of aura, see Gasché.

For DeLillo, whose use of the word 'aura' alludes in part to Benjamin's, the aesthetic contemplation formerly associated with the unique, authentic work of art, now appears, in a form at once attenuated and baleful, in the world of the instantaneous and reproducible televisual image. But the word 'aura', for DeLillo, also seems to include connotations drawn from the realm of spiritualism, alluding to the strange, coloured glow certain gifted souls claim to see around the outline of individuals. In DeLillo's work, the imaginary glow of the aura that surrounds a celebrity, for instance, is an indication, not of their inner qualities, but of their fame, the charge they carry in the eerily-lit world of the mass media. Aura, in this sense, is an index not of the celebrity's uniqueness, as such, but of their reproducibility, or, more accurately, of their uniqueness *as* reproducible. In one strand of *Mao II*, this curious structure of uniqueness-through-reproducibility points to the celebrity culture that impinges on the novelist Bill Gray, and, in another, it touches on the notion of subjectivity as something reproducible in the form of a kind of crowd-subject, the 'nonindividual' (70), an avatar of Poe's 'Man of the Crowd' for the mass media age, a figure who is both the antithesis and counterpart of the celebrity. In the figure of Karen Janney, the novel tries to imagine a strange new kind of subjectivity, one that emerges ominously from this peculiar shape that culture and experience have assumed at the end of the century.

II

The first chapter of *Mao II* opens with Bill Gray's amanuensis, Scott Martineau, browsing in a Manhattan bookstore. The narrative proper thus begins by exploring the site where literary and commercial concerns meet. Here Scott encounters the book-as-commodity, a libidinally and financially invested amalgam of literary production, image-management, and modern marketing technique:

> He looked at the gleaming best-sellers. People drifted through the store appearing caught in some unhappy dazzlement. There were books on step ladders and Lucite wall-shelves, books in pyramids and theme displays. He went downstairs to the paperbacks, where he stared at the covers of mass-market books, running his fingers erotically over the raised lettering. Covers were lacquered and gilded. Books lay cradled in nine-unit counterpacks like experimental babies. He could hear them shrieking *Buy me*. (19)

Scott's tour through the bookstore is a tour through a series of semiotically distinguished market sectors, from the lurid raised lettering on the covers of the best-sellers, to the 'austere umbers and rusts' (20) of Bill Gray's own highly regarded literary novels. Such discriminations remain – as much as the cunningly arrayed books in their 'artful fanning patterns' and 'little gothic snuggeries' (19), the photographs of authors prominently displayed, and the posters advertising books fairs and book weeks – part of a complex mechanism of publicity and retail designed to facilitate the exchange of commodities for cash. The relationship between writer and reader, mediated in this elaborate way by the various branches of the industry, assumes the inevitable stridency, likened to infantile demand, of the commodity's *Buy me*. Nice distinctions between author, image and text are elided in the process. 'Book and writer are now inseparable' (68), Scott later asserts. For this reason, he argues that Bill's *magnum opus*, on which the novelist has laboured more than twenty years, need not be published at all – Brita Nilsson's portrait photographs can take the book's place. 'We don't need the book,' he says. 'We have the author' (71).

It is this structure, rather than his self-elected privacy, which imprisons Bill Gray, ultimately rendering his struggles to engage with a world of political action an irrelevance. When Bill dies anonymously on board a ferry bound for Beirut, where he hopes to make contact with the terrorist group that has taken a Swiss poet hostage, Scott keeps hold of the manuscript, and plans to release Brita's photographs instead. The literal death of the author does nothing in this instance to liberate text or reader; rather, it confirms the dominance of the culture of image and celebrity. The possible public address of the novel, its capacity in Bill's words to 'alter the inner life of the culture' (41), remains only in the inverted and ironic form of refusal, silence, privacy. As Scott puts it: 'the withheld work of art is the only eloquence left' (67). On the face of it, this strategy seems to refine the Joycean dictum of silence, exile and cunning, but it turns out in *Mao II* to be a way of promoting authorial repute and garnering an additional value for an exclusive set of photographs. When the photographs finally appear, after Bill's death, they will cause a stir that outstrips any possible impact the book might have had, since the culture of celebrity which he resisted for so long has replaced the culture of literacy on which he long ago expended all his energy.

But the culture of celebrity is not restricted to those in the limelight. In *Mao II* it has acquired a universality, such that everyone is a subject of the media. As Bill Gray is photographed, early in the novel, he delivers a running commentary:

Everything around us tends to channel our lives toward some final reality in print or on film. Two lovers quarrel in the back of a taxi and a question becomes implicit in the event. Who will write the book and who will play the lovers in the movie? Everything seeks its own heightened version. Or put it this way. Nature has given way to aura. A man cuts himself shaving and someone is signed up to write a biography of the cut. All the material in every life is channeled into the glow. Here I am in your lens. Already I see myself differently. Twice over or once removed. (43–4)

These remarks point to a confusion of realms: the event and its representation, the private and the public, the self and the spectacle. Bill's examples suggest that a certain self-consciousness inhabits the most commonplace event, just as it shapes the subjectivity of the most ordinary person. Such self-consciousness has a teleological structure; it involves imagining a 'final reality in print or on film', a 'heightened version', a glossy and perfected representation beside which the original appears no more than a pretext or a degraded version. At the same time, this sense of a reality etiolated by the representations that haunt it also seems to involve an alarmingly close scrutiny, an intensified gaze levelled at the minutiae of everyday life. Whose gaze is this? In the context of Bill's remarks, the gaze is that of Brita Nilsson's camera. But her lens stands in for a general scopic anxiety, a sense that the ubiquitous image culture entails a corresponding surveillance. Another way of expressing this unease and confusion is in terms of a transformation of the meaning of the public and the private. On the one hand, private, intimate moments are now shaped by mass media images; on the other, the only way in which the public nature of the realm of publicity can be imagined is in terms of an invasive scrutiny.

An important exchange between Scott and Brita is informed by this sense of uncertain boundaries:

She said, 'In some places where you eat standing up you are forced to look directly into a mirror. This is total control of a person's responses, like a consumer prison. And the mirror is literally inches away so you can hardly put the food in your mouth without hitting into it.'

'The mirror is for safety, for protection. You use it to hide. You're totally alone in the foreground but you're also part of the swarm, the shifting jelly of heads looming over your little face.' (88–9)

For Brita, the mirror operates like a panoptic device, a mechanism that forces the subject into a disabling self-scrutiny, a self-enforced 'total control'. It is as if the mirror forces the person before it to assume a viewpoint of surveillance from behind its surface; in other words, the 'prisoner' identifies with a gaze that seems to originate from a spot in a room on the other side of the mirror (rather as if the mirror has a false back). The person before the mirror does all the work of regulation, placing him or herself implacably in the grip of the Other's gaze. For Scott, by contrast, the mirror is a blessing, since it offers a place to hide in an otherwise exposed public space. It seems to provide a sliding perspective, whereby one may be alone, unthreatened by the crowd, not overlooked in any way, while at the same time having the opportunity to mingle with the swarming mass. Anonymity, for Scott, is secured in both positions, whether one chooses to be faceless in the crowd, or faceless alone in the foreground. In this sense, for Scott the proximity of the mirror in a public place represents a relief from the burden of self-consciousness; and for this reason he connects what Brita calls a 'consumer prison' with mass-marriage: 'Bill doesn't understand how people need to blend in, lose themselves in something larger. The point of mass marriage is to show that we have to survive as a community instead of individuals trying to master every complex force' (89).

Mao II vividly imagines its characters caught in a restless movement between scrutiny and facelessness, the consumer prison and the crowd. There is 'thin-boundaried' (119) Karen, who absorbs the messages circulating in the culture and Unification Church doctrine with the same sense of rapture, who is 'lost in the dusty light' of television news, who has a feeling that she is 'involved not just in the coverage but in the terror' (117), and who watches footage of the Ayatollah Khomeini's funeral and wonders 'why is nothing changed, where are the local crowds, why do we still have names and addresses and car keys' (191). But coexisting with this heightened sense of identification – an identification with the nameless throng – is also a fantasy of complete isolation, the notion that 'she was the only one seeing this and everyone else tuned to this channel was watching sober-sided news analysis delivered by three men in a studio with makeup and hidden mikes' (190). The fantasy that the world is organised especially for the isolated self is akin to paranoia, and this in turn is a facet of Karen's consciousness: 'Every time she heard a creak in the floor she thought it was an armed attack. Always on the nameless alert' (142). She tells Scott 'If people knew what I was thinking they would put me away for ever'. To which he replies: 'But they would put us all away. We are put away for our thoughts, one way or another' (142).

Brita Nilsson's fear is that what she is thinking is altogether too public. On an airplane she has the sense 'that everything that came into her mind lately and developed as a perception seemed at once to enter the culture, to become a painting or photograph or hairstyle or slogan' (165). Her feeling that 'the world was so intimate that she was everywhere in it' (167) is a hairbreadth from a nightmare of proximity, where the attenuated boundaries of the self prove vulnerable to the flood of images, discourses, and fantasies that constitute the culture, the 'white noise' of the mass media that threatens to drown out anything distinctive in the self. This, at any rate, is the subtext of a series of discussions Bill Gray has with George Haddad, the academic who represents the terrorist group in Beirut, and with whom Bill is hesitantly dealing in his quixotic attempt to free the Swiss hostage. For Bill, the texture of distinctive writing serves as a token of the singularity of the self, a guarantee of identity; as he tells Brita, earlier in the novel 'I've always seen myself in sentences. I begin to recognize myself, word by word, as I work through a sentence' (48). This notion underwrites Bill's argument that the novel, with its many voices, its ambiguities and contradictions, is a model of democracy. The novel, he tells George Haddad, is 'a democratic shout' (159) which George's autocratic politics would wish to silence, just as they have silenced the hostage in his cell.

Mao II's movement from the spatial emblem to the dark cultural vision is more plausible than the subsequent step from the cultural to the political realm. To determine the reasons for this, and ultimately for the ethnocentric bias McClure detects, it is necessary to look at the foundation for the claims Bill Gray makes. *Mao II* has the problem that the only model for a democratic polity it can conjure up is the novel, a form that must stand in for a decidedly absent public space; the recognition of the inadequacy of this metaphor is to be felt in the arguments Bill has with George Haddad. Pressed to fight his corner, Bill retreats with the remark: 'I'm not a great big visionary, George. I'm a sentence-maker, like a donut-maker only slower' (162). This recourse to an artisanal metaphor betrays the weakness of the attempt to elaborate a claim for the democratic on the basis of the novel's unmediated artefactual status. To extend the claim for the democracy of the novel it would be necessary to take some account of the conditions of its reception, but here the analysis runs up against the vivid and thoroughgoing account of the commodification of literary culture. The relationship between the singularity of the individual and the faceless-ness of the crowd is a recapitulation of that between the author and a mass cultural public. For the perceived threat to the novel from autocratic political movements, which Bill tries quixotically to stage by setting out to meet the terrorist leader, is a displacement of the threat to this particular idea of the novel from the prevalent celebrity culture. In this respect, *Mao II* repeats the tiresome manoeuvre of desiring open political repression to contest; the bad faith of this desire is only too apparent. Considerably more compelling is the connection the novel makes between the crowd and the catastrophe, which is at once a diagnosis of the marginalization of the novel and an account of a special kind of mass cultural formation.

For if there is one phenomenon in DeLillo's vision of contemporary culture that has a force and primacy equal to that of the celebrity aura, it is the filmed disaster. The filmed disaster has an extraordinary capacity to grip, shape and dominate the cultural imagination. *White Noise* first brings this notion into prominence in DeLillo's work, depicting an environment saturated with media images of both celebrities and disasters, a culture besotted with and beset by catastrophe. Jack Gladney, the Professor of Hitler Studies at the College-on-the-Hill (his discipline illustrates the abiding fascination with extreme notoriety and catastrophe, as well as the dark humour typical of the book) makes a point of watching television with his family on Friday evenings, a duty enlivened on one memorable occasion by a compilation of disaster footage:

> There were floods, earthquakes, mud slides, erupting volcanoes. We'd never before been so attentive to our duty, our Friday assembly. Heinrich was not sullen, I was not bored. Steffie . . . appeared totally absorbed in these documentary clips of calamity and death. Babette tried to switch to a comedy series about a group of racially mixed kids who build their own communications satellite. She was startled by the force of our objection. We were otherwise silent, watching houses slide into the ocean, whole villages crackle and ignite in the mass of advancing lava. Every disaster made us wish for more, for something bigger, grander, more sweeping. (*White Noise*, 64)

The depiction of a progressive, liberal use of mass communications technology – the wholesome sitcom about racially mixed children building a satellite – has little of the appeal of disaster footage. Disasters have the effect of inciting a desire for the disastrous in a spiral of excess, founding a community of fascination on this dynamic. The lure of the cataclysmic offers a negative image of the medium, confirming the worst fears about television that Jack and his wife Babette set out to dispel with the Friday assembly, the spectre of a 'narcotic undertow and eerie diseased brain-sucking power' (*White Noise*, 16). Jack turns to his colleagues in the department of 'American environments' for an explanation, and is told that catastrophes help to relieve the jaded senses by interrupting the usual fluid operation of the medium; but at the same time, disasters confirm the power and ubiquity of television, giving a strong sense to the word 'coverage', and demonstrating that the technology is present even at scenes of social and natural upheaval. 'Nothing terrible escapes [the cameras'] scrutiny' (*White Noise*, 66), Jack is informed. The pleasure of watching a disaster arises in part, the argument runs, from knowing 'we're not missing anything' (*White Noise*, 66). There is, in other words, an implied identification between the avid interest of the viewer and the all-encompassing scrutiny of the television cameras, an identification of desire and technology.

For the novelist Bill Gray, the culture's fascination with catastrophes has relegated the novel to a position of disabling marginality. Scott explains:

> Bill has the idea that writers are being consumed by the emergence of news as an apocalyptic force. . . . The novel used to feed our search for meaning. Quoting Bill. It was the great secular transcendence. The Latin mass of language, character, occasional new truth. But our desperation has led us toward something larger and darker. So we turn to the news, which provides an unremitting mood of catastrophe. This is where we find emotional experience not available elsewhere. We don't need the novel. Quoting Bill. We don't even need catastrophes, necessarily. We only need reports and predictions and warnings. (72)

Bill Gray's idea firmly places the catastrophe at the centre of contemporary culture. Doom and its prognostication supplies the present with 'the unchanged narrative every culture needs in order to survive' (162). 'News of disaster is the only narrative people need,' (42) Bill Gray tells the photographer Brita Nilsson. This narrative is the ground of collectivity. While Scott's paraphrase of Bill's thoughts does little to explain the emotional appeal of apocalyptic news, suggesting only that an indeterminate desperation demands a certain corresponding extremity and darkness, the passage does, nevertheless, emphasize the collective nature of that appeal, the cultural dominance of the mood of catastrophe. The novelist cannot participate in this apocalyptic culture, in part, the novel argues, because fiction is too fine-grained to make any impression on a culture dominated by the news medium's mode of excess. Only terrorists, Bill Gray claims, can exploit the nexus of disaster and media coverage which now occupies the centre of contemporary culture. 'The darker the news, the grander the narrative,' Bill stresses. 'News is the last addiction before – what? I don't know' (42).

Bill's analysis of the appeal of catastrophes is itself an apocalyptic narrative – a sensational tale of the eclipse of a cultural formation, a story of decadence and extinctions. What follows the end? Bill, of course, can have no answer, but he remarks on the timeliness of Brita Nilsson's project, a photographic census, so to speak, of writers across the globe: 'you're smart to trap us in your camera before we disappear' (42). Bill's apocalyptic narrative gives an ironic twist to the often celebratory postmodern announcement of the demise of the grand narratives of the Enlightenment, those stories of the modern age which saw scientific, cultural and societal progress as directed towards the emancipation of humanity.[8] It is possible to extrapolate from Bill Gray's remarks, and indeed, from the novel as a whole, in order to argue that the hunger for grand narratives of decline and fall testifies to the weakening of grand narratives of progress, but not to any subsequent weakening of a desire for narrative as such. But, of course, the dark, apocalyptic narratives were always already implicit in the sunnier Enlightenment stories of progress and emancipation as their obverse, emerging at times of anxiety over social change. DeLillo's own story of dark addictions and promised endings falls within a distinguished lineage of apocalyptic American writing, which includes in the twentieth century Henry Adams, Nathanael West, and William Gaddis. In Mao II, the anxiety over social change takes the form of an 'inertia-hysteria' of the crowd, where the public is frozen into the image of a transaction between commodities and cultural consumers, a consumer prison, on the one hand, and an image of reproducibility, or facelessness, on the other. These two faces of the crowd point to the profound unthinkability of a collective future. The best emblem of this – an emblem that appears tragic and affectless at the same time – is finally supplied by one of Warhol's silkscreens, examined by Scott:

> The walls looked off to heaven in a marvelous flat-eyed gaze. He stood before a silk screen called Crowd. The image was irregular, deep streaks marking the canvas, and it seemed to him that the crowd itself, the vast mesh of people, was being riven by some fleeting media catastrophe. (20–1)

---

[8] This is the controversial claim of Lyotard (1984).

Afflicted or fragmented by catastrophe, the crowd's gaze is flat-eyed because it has lost the ability to see. It remains transfixed before the lurid disaster of the screen, beyond which no future is visible.

Works Cited

Benjamin, Walter, 1973. 'The Work of Art in the Age of Mechanical Repro-
    duction,' *Illuminations*, trans. Harry Zohn, London: Fontana, 219–53.
DeLillo, Don, 1982. *The Names*, New York: Knopf.
———, 1985. *White Noise*, New York: Viking.
———, 1991. *Mao II*, New York: Viking.
Emerson, Ralph Waldo, 1990. 'Nature' (1836). *Ralph Waldo Emerson (The Oxford Authors)*, ed. Richard Poirier, Oxford: Oxford University Press.
Evans, Kim, (dir.), 1991. 'Don DeLillo: The Word, The Image and The Gun', broadcast BBC 1, 27 September.
Frow, John, 1990. ' "The Last Things Before the Last": Notes on *White Noise*' *South Atlantic Quarterly* 89, 237–98.
Gasché, Rodolphe, 1994. 'Objective Diversions: On Some Kantian Themes in Benjamin's "The Work of Art in the Age of Mechanical Reproduction" ', *Walter Benjamin's Philosophy: Destruction and Experience*, ed. Andrew Benjamin and Peter Osborne. London: Routledge, 183–204.
Jameson, Fredric, 1991. *Postmodernism: or, The Cultural Logic of Late Capitalism*, London: Verso.
Le Bon, Gustave, 1960. *The Crowd: A Study of the Popular Mind*, no translator named, New York: Viking.
Lyotard, Jean-François, 1984. *The Postmodern Condition: A Report on Knowledge*, trans. Geoff Bennington and Brian Massumi, Minneapolis: Minnesota University Press.
McClure, John, 1994. *Late Imperial Romance*, London: Verso.

Notes on Contributors

Margaret Beetham is Senior Lecturer and Course Leader of the Women's Studies M.A. in the Department of English and History at the Manchester metropolitan University. She co-authored *Women's Worlds: Ideology, Femininity and the Women's Magazine* (Macmillan, 1991) and has published on nineteenth-century periodicals, feminist theory, and pedagogy. *A Magazine of Her Own?: Domesticity and Desire in the Woman's Magazine* is due out from Routledge in early 1996.

Laurel Brake is Senior Lecturer in Literature at Birkbeck College, University of London. Author of *Subjegated Knowledges: Journalism, Gender, and Literature in the Nineteenth Century* (Macmillan, 1994) and *Walter Pater* (Northcote House, 1994), she has edited *The Year's Work in English Studies* (1981–7), and co-edited *Investigating Victorian Journalism* (Macmillan, 1990) and *Pater in the 1990s* (ELT Press, 1991). She is working on a full-length biography of Pater.

Joseph Bristow is Senior Lecturer in English at the University of York, where he is also affiliated with the Centre for Women's Studies. Among his recent publications are a New Casebook, *Victorian Women Poets: Emily Bronte, Elizabeth Barrett Browning and Christina Rossetti*, and *Effeminate England: Homoerotic Writing after 1855*. He is currently completing a full-length study entitled 'Victorian Poems, Victorian Sexualities.'

Jeremy Green is an Assistant Professor in the Department of English at the University of Arizona, Tucson. He is currently working on a full-length study of the fiction of Don DeLillo.

Gordon McMullan is a Lecturer in English Literature at King's College, London. His publications include *The Politics of Unease in the Plays of John Fletcher* (Massachusetts, 1994) and a co-edited collection, *The Politics of Tragicomedy: Shakespeare and After* (Routledge, 1992). He is currently editing Shakespeare and Fletcher's *Henry VIII* for Arden III.

Penny Smith is a Lecturer in English in the Deptartment of Historical and Critical Studies at the University of Northumbria at Newcastle where she teaches contemporary writing and creative writing. She is currently doing research on regional Northern writing, and has published short stories and two novels, *The End of April* and *Crosswords* (Women's Press), under the name of Penny Sumner.

Helen Wilcox is Professor of English Literature and Head of the Department of English at the University of Groningen, the Netherlands. Her publications include *Her Own Life: Autobiographical Writing by 17th Century Englishwomen* (1989), *George Herbert, Sacred and Profane* (1995), and *Women and Literature in Britain 1500–1700* (1996), and she is editor of the forthcoming Longman's Annotated George Herbert. Her current research activity includes writing a book on the seventeenth-century devotional lyric and editing *All's Well That Ends Well*.